ADVANCE PRAISE FOR

REASONS MOMMY DRINKS

"The ultimate baby shower gift."
—Author's sister

"It's the must-have for new Moms."
—Paid PR person

"This book is destined to become an Emmy award–
winning sitcom."
—Authors' agent

"Even new fathers will appreciate this book. Buy multiple copies!"
—Publisher

"I'm so glad I took my birth control this morning."
—Single girl

REASONS MOMMY DRINKS

Lyranda Martin Evans

and Fiona Stevenson

THREE RIVERS PRESS · NEW YORK

Published in the United States by Three Rivers Press, an imprint
of the Crown Publishing Group, a division of Random House, Inc.,
New York.
www.crownpublishing.com

Three Rivers Press and the Tugboat design are registered
trademarks of Random House, Inc.

Portions of this work first appeared on the authors' blog
ReasonsMommyDrinks.com.

Library of Congress Cataloging-in-Publication Data
Martin Evans, Lyranda.
Reasons mommy drinks / Lyranda Martin Evans and Fiona
Stevenson.—First edition.
pages cm
1. Parenthood—Humor. 2. Child rearing—Humor. I. Stevenson,
Fiona. II. Title.
PN6231.P2M345 2013
818'.602—dc23
2013017870

ISBN 978-0-385-34929-1
eISBN 978-0-385-34930-7

Printed in the United States of America

Book design by Maria Elias
Logo design and pacifier illustrations by Moira Stevenson
Layout art direction and stemware illustrations by Travis Cowdy
Cover design by Travis Cowdy
Cover photography by Vicky Lam
Author photograph by Gustavo Gonzalez

10 9 8 7 6 5 4 3 2 1

First Edition

This book is dedicated to our amazing children, who bring endless joy to our hearts. We truly didn't know this kind of happiness was possible before you were born. When you read this book when you're older, may you not seek immediate emancipation, knowing it in no way relates to your childhood. Now over to our lawyers for more on that:

See? That's the law talking. You can't argue with that. So no using this book as an excuse for teenage angst or as blackmail to get us to buy you a flying space car or whatever. By the way, we really hope all this legalese is inspiring you to consider a career in law (or business or medicine). Because as the Ancient Romans used to say, *Faber est quisque fortunae suae.* Translation: Don't go into the arts.

CONTENTS

Introduction • 15

The baby shower • 18

Prenatal class • 20

Labor • 22

Trying not to break you • 24

Naming you • 26

Nursing • 28

The nursery • 30

She couldn't drink for
nine months • 32

Visitors • 34

Mommy and Me movies • 36

The car seat • 38

Mommy groups • 40

She can't *drink* drink • 42

The spa • 44

Wearing you • 46

No more pregnancy perks • 48

She can't take a sick day • 50

Sex • 52

Lack of sleep • 54

The office visit • 56

Her hair is falling out • 58

The in-laws • 60

Celebrity moms • 62

Celebrity babies • 64

Labor in the movies • 66

Everything makes her cry • 68

The diaper bag • 70

Public transportation • 72

Explosive poo • 74

You're sick • 76

Mommy brain • 78

Baby Gap • 80

Plastic toys • 82

Mommy and Me yoga • 84

Sleep training • 86

The family pet • 88

Ex-boyfriends • 90

The weather • 92

TV • 94

Facebook • 96

Global warming • 98

Swim class • 100

Flying • 102

Real estate • 104

She's asymmetrical • 106

The growth spurt • 108

The babysitter • 110

Diapers • 112

Nap time • 114

Hotels • 116

The laundry • 118

Home renovations • 120

The end of maternity leave • 122

The pump • 124

The business trip • 126

Wardrobe • 128

Disposable income • 130

Brunch • 132

Holidays • 134

The Nanny • 136

Daddy • 138

"When are you having a
second?" • 140

Single people • 142

Bath time • 144

Meal planning • 146

You're a hair puller • 148

Photography • 150

The pediatrician • 152

Baby proofing • 154

Your first birthday • 156

Weaning • 158

Your first haircut • 160

Sippy cups • 162

Gadgets • 164

Teething • 166

Board books • 168

Grocery shopping • 170

Working from home • 172

9 PM • 174

The gym membership • 176

First steps • 178

Compulsively checking on you
while you sleep • 180

The park • 182

Accelerated aging • 184

The stroller • 186

Sports • 188

Grandma • 190

Day care • 192

Houseguests • 194

Mommy Fear • 196

The Playdate • 198

Children's music • 200

Restaurants • 202

Mornings • 204

Weddings • 206

Other kids • 208

Other Mommies • 210

Mommy nights out • 212

Vacations • 214

You're growing up too fast • 216

Acknowledgments • 218

Index • 220

REASONS MOMMY DRINKS

INTRODUCTION

If you're a new mother reading this, it's probably 3 AM and your nipples are bleeding. Welcome!

Even if you've been a parent for years or you're toying with the idea of becoming one, we hope you enjoy this journey through the first eighteen months of new motherhood. It's a beautiful baby story set to the soft musical notes of Sarah McLachlan, only the exact opposite. No one tells you that on some days you're going to wonder, *What the hell have I done?* And then feel all guilty about wondering that. Then, five minutes later, all is bliss again because you see that first newborn smile. Which is gas, but it's desperate times in those early days so take whatever moments you can get.

Creative liberties were taken—obviously the section about Grandma is a complete joke and in no way based in fact (*cough*)— and the drink recipes (while delicious!) should be enjoyed in moderation. You're a mom now. You have to be the responsible one. You might as well toss your low-cut sequin halter because the days of flirting with the bartender to get your French martini on the house are over. But, good news: Being a mother is the Greatest Job in the World. We promise. It really, really is. Oh, there will still be days that make you want to pack it all in and go Thelma and Louise off a cliff, but those are also the days that yield the comedic gold. We hope you laugh along with us, covered in baby barf, and cherish every moment.

And by the way, chances are you rock as a mom. Even on the days you feel like you're failing, you're probably doing a stellar job. We all go through this. Let's go through it together.

With the occasional after-the-kids-have-gone-to-bed cocktail.

PACIFIER RATING SYSTEM

Baby brain can make it hard for a mother to figure out what she needs. Cue this handy Pacifier Rating System, set on a scale from one to five for easy reference on how badly the cocktail accompanying each reason is needed. **Note:** The rating does not indicate the *number* of drinks needed, but rather how badly *a* drink is needed after baby's bedtime. Mommy is not a hillbilly.

RATING SCALE

The drink may be required.
Or try using Sophie the Giraffe as a stress ball.

The drink is probably necessary, paired with carbs,
chocolate, and threadbare sweatpants.

The drink is a must. Serve in the least crud-encrusted
stemware or sippy cup on hand.

Something gross was probably sprayed on you.
Prepare drink immediately. Chase with a hot shower.

Situation critical! Code Johnnie Walker Red!
Get a cocktail shaker and an IV line stat!

THE BABY SHOWER

The baby shower is a painful rite of passage, cleverly disguised with adorable pink or blue ribbons that later become an embarrassing hat. Well-educated, properly raised, successful women resort to eating baby food, guessing how fat Mommy is, and melting Oh Henry! bars in diapers to simulate poo. The other Mommies in the room share heartwarming labor anecdotes ("I ripped all the way to my asshole!") while the single girls silently curse the fact that there's never any booze at these things and make mental notes never to forget to take their birth control again. For some reason, Daddy isn't subjected to the baby shower, unless you consider a couple of guys from work taking him to Hooters "for the wings" a celebration of your upcoming birth. Mommy really got the raw end (but no raw sushi!) of this deal. Though she is grateful for the generous gifts, she wishes she could have been as tipsy as she was at her bridal shower to help her feign enthusiasm when unwrapping Udderly Smooth: for cracked, bleeding nipples.

THE DUE DATE

(nonalcoholic)

INGREDIENTS

½ cup pitted dates

½ cup strawberries

1 cup orange juice

1 banana

1½ ounces maple syrup

INSTRUCTIONS

Combine all the ingredients with cracked ice in
a blender and blend until smooth. Enjoy during
Braxton Hicks.

HOW BADLY YOU NEED THIS DRINK

PRENATAL CLASS

Mommy was obviously high on folic acid when she decided to spend her final pre-baby days in a hospital basement, role-playing labor scenarios. The class begins with icebreakers. Mommy's not sure what's more uncomfortable: your foot pressing against her bladder or watching Daddy compete for the title of wittiest heckler. The fun and games end when a graphic vaginal birth unfolds before Daddy's eyes, courtesy of a Betamax tape circa 1977. Mommy suspects Daddy regrets the egg salad sandwich he purchased from the hospital cafeteria, which is confirmed when she sees him swallow a mouthful of vomit. *Ooooh, here comes more awkward tomfoolery!* The middle-aged instructor drops to the floor to dramatize her own labor experience and contorts her floral-printed palazzo pants into a pretzel-like formation over her head while chanting a Buddhist mantra. Mommy should be taking copious notes about what to do when her first contraction hits, but she's on a pleasure cruise down a river called De Nial. Fact: She spends a large portion of the class having name fights with Daddy via text. In hindsight, prenatal class was a colossal waste of money as literally nothing about your birth went according to plan. See next entry.

BABY BELLY-NI

(nonalcoholic)

INGREDIENTS

5 ounces chilled sparkling nonalcoholic cider

2 ounces peach nectar

Splash of lemon juice

INSTRUCTIONS

Chill a Champagne flute. Pour in all the ingredients, stir, and enjoy your final days of freedom. You have no idea.

HOW BADLY YOU NEED THIS DRINK

LABOR

After two decades of training cramps, it's time to put Mommy's pain tolerance to the ultimate test. The Marathon of Pain begins when Mommy's water breaks, flooding her Heidi Klum Under Belly leggings and leading her to scream, "Is this actually happening?" as if the excruciating pain consuming her whole body wasn't clue enough. Meanwhile, the masterful contraction-timing techniques that Daddy picked up from YouTube elude him in the heat of the moment. He does manage to locate the four least important items from Mommy's extensive hospital packing list before cramming her gargantuan belly into the car. Within five minutes of triage, Mommy's eighteen-step birth plan (which included barring med students from her vagina and playing Enya on repeat) goes down the drain, as does the goat cheese and mushroom wrap she ate for lunch. Following the advice of her doula, she's opted for a natural childbirth,* so Mommy screams her way through eight hours of *Zero Dark Thirty* torture, much to the horror of the entire B wing. At one point, she begs for the epidural, but Daddy gently reminds her of their natural, pharma-free strategy. Mommy tries to murder Daddy with her bare hands. The rest is a complete blackout from her memory, which is apparently nature's way of ensuring that women procreate again. The truth is that if Mommies could accurately remember and retell the ripping, the spilling of bodily fluids, and the tearing from tip to tail, the whole human race would cease to exist.

---

* To all expectant Moms: Don't be a hero. Take the drugs. Take the goddamned drugs.

THE "WISH YOU WERE A" VIRGIN MARY

(nonalcoholic)

INGREDIENTS

4 ounces tomato juice

1 ounce lime juice

¼ teaspoon horseradish

Tabasco sauce to taste

Worcestershire sauce to taste

Pinch of salt

Pinch of freshly ground pepper

Wedge of lime

INSTRUCTIONS

Fill a glass with the tomato and lime juices. Add the horseradish, Tabasco, Worcestershire, salt, and pepper and stir. Garnish with a lime wedge. Serve over ice chips.

HOW BADLY YOU NEED THIS DRINK

TRYING NOT TO
BREAK YOU

And so you are born. Mommy had pictured a Circle of Life moment, scored by Elton John, in which you would gracefully whoosh into the world. In truth, the whole thing was a shit show. Yet somehow you are perfect and unscathed. Now it's Mommy and Daddy's job not to break you. You weigh less than Mommy's Marc Jacobs tote, and once the doctors and nurses leave the room, Mommy and Daddy give each other a blank stare that conveys that neither of them has any idea what to do next. The nurses pop in to manhandle you, and while it causes Mommy and Daddy unadulterated panic, you seem alarmingly unfazed by it all. Leaving the hospital is terrifying. Mommy is crippled by the fear that she's going to drop you, fail to support your head, or say something permanently scarring to Daddy like "Send it back!" It's also a challenge because it takes one hour to buckle you into the car seat and another hour to cautiously travel the 2.8 miles home.

Now they're home. Alone. FUUUUUUUUUUCK. They worry that although they wash their hands compulsively, the Ebola virus is too strong for Bath & Body Works. They worry every gurgle is a sign you're choking and within the first forty-eight hours call 911 twice. They worry the black stuff oozing out of you is actually your inner organs. They watch you sleep; they watch you breathe; they cradle you gently and pray to God they're doing it right. Or at least not doing it *totally* wrong.

STARBUCKS
VIA INSTANT COFFEE

(nonalcoholic)

NOTE

Buy a whole case. You're going to need it.

HOW BADLY YOU NEED THIS DRINK

el NAMING YOU le

Naming you was one of the more stressful things about being pregnant. After all, your name is your brand. Mommy had lists and lists written in notebooks, on Post-its, and in 4,987 emails to Daddy. What name would her friends say judgmental things about behind her back? What would look good on the ballot for president and in no way sound like it belongs to a stripper? What would work best with Daddy's last name? Ugh, that's another thing. Mommy thinks it's archaic that babies almost automatically get their fathers' last names. She considered hyphenating your last name, but unless you're British royalty, it sounds pretentious. Actually, even then it sounds pretentious. Plus, when Mommy mentioned it to Daddy, he mumbled something about pregnancy hormones and went and got her cheese fries at 4 AM, and she promptly dropped the whole thing. Ultimately, when it came to naming you, Daddy chimed in with helpful suggestions like "I slept with a girl named that once," but it was Mommy who scoured the Nameberry website, every name book at Barnes & Noble, and the family tree and finally landed on the perfect moniker. Which Grandma and Grandpa hate.

THE BIRTH ANNOUNCEMENT

(nonalcoholic)

INGREDIENTS

1½ ounces raspberry syrup

4 ounces chilled sparkling nonalcoholic cider

INSTRUCTIONS

Chill a wine glass. Stir the syrup with cracked ice
in a mixing glass and pour into the wine glass. Fill
with the apple cider and stir gently. Forget muddling
over your narrowed-down list of 412 names and go
muddle some raspberries to make this mocktail even
more delicious.

HOW BADLY YOU NEED THIS DRINK

NURSING

Even though Mommy and 90 percent of her cohort grew up exclusively on formula and still manage to navigate life just fine, Mommy bowed to the pressure and decided to try her hand (well, actually, breast) at feeding you. The studies (with ten disclaimers) about improved brain development piqued her curiosity, but truth be told, it was the prospect of burning five hundred calories a day while parking herself in front of *Ellen* that sealed the deal. Not to mention the price tag of free. With serene stock photography images of nursing mothers and children from the hospital literature dancing in her head, Mommy was shocked to discover that the early days of breastfeeding can be even more painful than labor. Daddy has his own shockisode when he watches Mommy's breasts swell to triple Es the night her milk comes in. Although his arousal quickly subsides when your incorrect latch leaves Mommy's nipples looking like raw hamburger meat. Five trips to the lactation consultant and an $800 bill later, Mommy finally reaches a point where breast-feeding you doesn't feel like a thousand pins and needles being shoved into her nipples simultaneously. Looking down on you while you suckle yourself to sleep, she suddenly feels all Movie-of-the-Week emotional. Though she'll never admit it to Daddy (because she's still cashing in her bout with mastitis for back rubs and sleep-ins), Mommy thinks breast-feeding you is kind of awesome.

A PINT OF GUINNESS

NOTE

Though not supported by any empirical evidence
whatsoever, one glass is purported to help your
milk come in. Irish: 1, Science: 0.

HOW BADLY YOU NEED THIS DRINK

THE NURSERY

Mommy used to furnish her home with the perfect blend of high design and mid-century modern style. But your impending arrival drove her to throw all good taste out the (now flanked by teddy bear curtains) window. This psychotic break in good taste is called nesting, which is appropriate given the number of cutesy bird plush toys now strewn all over this once minimalist den. At first, Mommy had visions of geometric black-and-white sheets, one whimsical Blabla doll handmade in Peru, and a gorgeous Scandinavian rocking chair she saw on Pinterest. Then something terrible happened. She was overcome with the urge to paint the walls a seizure-inducing shade of chartreuse, frame hideously adorable ABC posters, and buy a safari-themed musical mobile that sounds eerily like the theme from *A Nightmare on Elm Street*. The final nail in the coffin for her dreams of a nursery worthy of *Architectural Digest* came when she took one look at the price tag of an Oeuf crib. Off to IKEA she went, followed by a shopping spree at Babies "R" Us. According to the twenty-two-year-old receptionist at her ob-gyn office, it's *critical* that your nursery has a theme. The theme of your room: Mommy Surrenders.

TEQUILA MOCKINGBIRD

INGREDIENTS

1 ounce tequila

3 ounces lemon-lime soda

Splash of cranberry juice

INSTRUCTIONS

Fill a glass with ice. Pour in all the ingredients
and stir. Make sure you nurse it.

HOW BADLY YOU NEED THIS DRINK

SHE COULDN'T DRINK
FOR NINE MONTHS

Mommy did the math and figured out you were conceived after she polished off a bottle of red with Daddy on an empty stomach. The throbbing headache made her slightly regret that at work the next day, but little did she know that this magical and blurry evening was her last hurrah for nine months. The minute she found out she was having you, she stopped drinking—and also gave up unpasteurized cheese, Diet Coke, coffee, sushi, and fun. Apparently in France women enjoy all of these things in moderation when they're pregnant, but Mommy couldn't handle the judgmental North American stares. Plus, all the conflicting literature on what's harmless and what's not during pregnancy made Mommy play it on the safe side, to put it mildly. This meant constantly complaining to security about the smokers outside her office tower, washing her hands every five minutes, popping prenatal vitamins like an addict, and eating an excessive amount of steamed kale. Mommy was now the Least Fun Person at Every Party, and she noticed her Evite invitations took a steep decline during this time. That was actually fine with her. The combination of nausea from morning sickness (inaccurately named because she had it *all the time*), extreme fatigue, and general disgust with maternity wardrobe options made her perfectly happy to RSVP her regrets. Of course, she wasn't always the picture of health; she probably spent a good chunk of your college fund on trips to DQ. Maybe that's why her ob-gyn, upon seeing the results on the scale, told her to "slow down." Unfortunately, this had the reverse effect, as Mommy later ate her feelings in the form of a Mint Oreo Blizzard.

CABERNET FRANC

INSTRUCTIONS

Now that you can have the occasional drink, enjoy
1 gorgeous glass paired with gooey, unpasteurized
Brie. *Vive la France!*

HOW BADLY YOU NEED THIS DRINK

‏‏‎ VISITORS ‏‎

Mommy just had her insides ripped apart and her entire world turned upside down, and has slept a combined total of seventeen minutes in the past week. The last thing she feels like doing, besides getting pregnant ever again, is turning her home into a revolving door for friends, neighbors, and distant cousins who think they're doing Mommy a favor by being among the very first human beings to meet you. Fresh off germy public transit or on their last round of antibiotics, they immediately want to pry you from Mommy's arms with their unwashed hands and inadequate neck-supporting techniques. Then Mommy is forced to play photographer, which involves multiple retakes and twenty minutes of postproduction work on an iPhone. Meanwhile, Daddy embraces the opportunity to entertain. "Beers for everyone!" Mommy wants nothing more than to crawl into bed and emerge when you can read, but instead she finds herself listening to Suzy No Kids's overly detailed account of a minimalist art exhibit while silently brainstorming strategies for cutting this visit short. Every visitor assumes maternity leave is one long vacation and thus expects lunch. As do you. Mommy is forced to further complicate the process of latching you to her painfully engorged breast by introducing a Hooter Hider into the mix while simultaneously grilling panini.

THE WARM WELCOME

INGREDIENTS

5 ounces apple cider

¾ ounce bourbon

¾ ounce apple liqueur

1 cinnamon stick

INSTRUCTIONS

Warm the apple cider on the stovetop and pour into a mug. Add the bourbon and apple liqueur, and stir. Garnish with a cinnamon stick. Do not serve to any visitors or they'll never leave.

HOW BADLY YOU NEED THIS DRINK

MOMMY AND
ME MOVIES

After weeks under house arrest, Mommy emerges into the bright lights of humanity and Hollywood to attend a Mommy and Me movie. Mommy is so desperate to go out she'll see anything, even a movie starring Anne Hathaway. A broken elevator and grueling half hour spent navigating your monster stroller through the parking lot's M. C. Escher stair system later, Mommy splurges on a bucket of buttery popcorn that immediately offsets any postpartum weight loss. The movie is already ten minutes in, but Mommy can't hear what's going on anyway over the Dolby digital surround-sound screeching of colicky babies, including you. Mommy spends the next 102-minute running time running up and down the aisles attempting to soothe you. Unfortunately, the moment you fall asleep coincides with the exact moment of an unexpected plot twist involving a massive explosion. This not only jolts you awake but also makes you shit your pants, forcing Mommy to line up for the communal change table lined with 312 strains of bacteria. Great news! With the lights left partially on, she can see you've actually shit on her. Mommy doesn't know who is most deserving of her sympathy: herself, the teenagers who didn't know it was Mommy and Me day and are hating life, or the one uncomfortable Dad in the crowd who is flanked by row upon row of exposed, engorged nipples. Roll credits.

THE SILVER SCREAM

INGREDIENTS

1 ounce Silver Patrón tequila

1½ ounces orange juice

1½ ounces grapefruit juice

1½ ounces cranberry juice

INSTRUCTIONS

Fill a glass with ice. Pour in all the ingredients and
stir.

NOTE

Pairs well with microwave popcorn and your
dusty DVD collection.

HOW BADLY YOU NEED THIS DRINK

THE CAR SEAT

Your cousin's outgrown car seat models were taking up prime storage space for five years before Mommy learned that car seats have expiration dates. Seriously? The Corolla in which it will be installed is one frost away from collapse, but apparently it's the gently used Britax Marathon that's obsolete. Time to spend another $200 on something you'll outgrow in less time than you spent in the womb. At least babies love going for a drive and immediately drift off to sleep when placed in a car seat. Except, for some reason, you. You scream like *Saw 4* is being filmed in the backseat for the entire ride. Not even Mommy's Madonna megamix can soothe you. Even though all the windows are rolled up, the other drivers can see your tears and are giving Mommy the "Bad Mother" glare. Unfortunately, she has to put you in the car seat to get to her Mommy groups, which are a whole other reason Mommy needs a drink.

THE SAFE TRAVELER

(nonalcoholic)

INGREDIENTS

2 ounces pear juice

2 ounces apple juice

Splash of lemon juice

Sage leaf

INSTRUCTIONS

Combine the pear, apple, and lemon juices in a shaker
with ice. Shake well and strain into an ice-filled glass.
Garnish with a sage leaf.

HOW BADLY YOU NEED THIS DRINK

MOMMY GROUPS

While on maternity leave, Mommy is forced to travel in unchartered social circles known as Mommy groups. Gatherings take place at rotating houses belonging to the other Mommies from her prenatal class. She would never normally socialize with most of these people, but all her real friends are working and Mommy is desperate. With babies either asleep in Graco car seats or suckling at breasts, most Mommy group sessions are giant bitchfests about latching problems, lack of sleep, and useless husbands. Mommy chronically forgets to pack the Hooter Hider before leaving home, which means pulling a Janet Jackson to quell your hunger squeals before they drown out Norah Jones. Mommy groups can be weirdly competitive. These women boast about their eight-week-old's above-average bowel movements and compare push gifts from Tiffany. Most of the women also insist on baking everything from scratch, and this poses a problem when it's Mommy's turn to host because she has no idea how an oven works. This quickly snowballs into a giant charade of buying gluten-free muffins at Whole Foods and burning all the evidence. Mommy is exhausted from pretending to be interested in their parenting styles ("My Liam is self-actualized!") and nanny searches ("Manuela has an early childhood education degree, but she's *from an island*"), but when faced with the alternative of social isolation and meals eaten out of a peanut butter jar, Mommy finds herself counting down the minutes until the next meeting.

THE STEPFORD SPRITZER

INGREDIENTS

Equal parts any boxed wine and Perrier

INSTRUCTIONS

Fill a glass with ice. Pour in the wine and Perrier, and stir.

HOW BADLY YOU NEED THIS DRINK

SHE CAN'T *DRINK* DRINK

Mommy used to party irresponsibly. She used to wear pleather and dance on the bar to "Pony" by Ginuwine, and once while overserved $2 Amaretto sours she ate a whole apple pie off some random dude's table. Mommy would wake up in a dry-mouthed haze at noon and piece together the evening through Facebook photos and a Sent folder of drunken texts to ex-boyfriends. Then she'd meet her friends for brunch at 2 PM to discuss who made out with which bouncer. Now if Mommy has more than a glass of wine she pays for it at 2 AM, 4 AM, and 6 AM, when you wake up screaming and she has to feed you from the stash of breast milk in the freezer. She used to keep nothing but vodka and an eye mask in there. Times have changed.

EIGHTEEN-YEAR-OLD GLENLIVET

INSTRUCTIONS

1 ounce, served neat. If you're going to have only one drink, make it count.

HOW BADLY YOU NEED THIS DRINK

THE SPA

On the occasion of Mommy's birthday, Daddy tries to melt away three months of emotional, mental, and physical exhaustion with the (previously) fail-safe gift of a day at the spa. Unfortunately, Mommy's first postnatal spa visit doesn't quite pan out as planned. First, the massage therapist has the misguided notion that Mommy wants to spend her first child-free hour in months answering a continuous stream of questions about labor when all she really wants to do is fantasize about Matt Damon. Mommy's rejuvenation facial is scored by pan flutes, wind chimes, and a lecture about the toll that her lack of sleep is taking on the skin around her eyes, delivered by an aesthetician who looks twelve. Mommy hasn't even cracked *Us Weekly* in the postservice tranquility room when Daddy calls with the news that you've been wailing incessantly for the past forty-five minutes, refusing to take the bottle. Mommy heads immediately to the checkout desk, where she's pressured in her vulnerable postpartum state into dropping $75 on an antigravity firming lift cream from France that she'll find unopened and expired in her bathroom drawer in 2020. As she races uptown at lightning speed, Mommy's nipples leak all over the steering wheel. Serenity now!

ZEN COCKTAIL

INGREDIENTS

½ ounce green tea liqueur

½ ounce melon liqueur

3 ounces mango juice

2 ounces cream

Fresh mint leaves

Freshly ground nutmeg

INSTRUCTIONS

Combine the green tea liqueur, melon liqueur, mango juice, and cream in a shaker with ice. Shake well and strain into a Champagne flute. Garnish with mint and nutmeg, and hold your breath for eighteen years.

HOW BADLY YOU NEED THIS DRINK

WEARING YOU

Even more hotly debated than health-care reform is which of the 563 models of baby-wearing devices to buy. Despite witnessing multiple demos by store clerks on some petrifying dummy babies, Mommy never actually mastered any of the three baby carriers she purchased during a hormone-induced shopping spree in her last trimester. There was the structured baby carrier from Europe with twelve buckles, six adjustment straps, and a recall notice. There was the two-foot-wide, sixteen-foot-long piece of organic cotton fabric that all the websites said was "so easy to use!" that Mommy almost strangled herself with. And finally there was the ergonomically designed backpack that was more difficult to assemble than an IKEA EXPEDIT shelving unit. Mommy was forced to resort to the "idiot-proof" online instructional videos after your birth, but they were far too complex for her sleep-deprived brain. After three months of carrying you in her arms every waking minute of the day, Mommy finally struck gold with a borrowed sling that looks like a cross between Joseph's Technicolor Dreamcoat and the wallpaper in her great aunt's bathroom. Mommy is now a prime candidate for *What Not to Wear: Maternal Edition,* but at least she can finally make a sandwich with two hands.

SINGAPORE SLING

INGREDIENTS

½ ounce grenadine

1 ounce gin

2 ounces sweet-and-sour mix

2 ounces chilled club soda

½ ounce cherry brandy

Cherry

INSTRUCTIONS

Pour the grenadine into the bottom of a glass and fill
with ice. Add the gin, sweet-and-sour mix, and club
soda. Top with the cherry brandy, stir, and garnish
with a cherry.

HOW BADLY YOU NEED THIS DRINK

NO MORE PREGNANCY PERKS

Sure, there are a lot of things Mommy doesn't miss about being pregnant. Like heartburn, cankles, and three months spent hugging the toilet bowl. But pregnancy definitely had its pluses. Aside from the forty pounds of extra weight around her midsection, Mommy-to-be was a spitting image of a Victoria Secret model thanks to her double-D rack, luscious locks, and hormone-charged glow. Armed with her "baby brain" pass, she never had to sweat forgetting a best friend's birthday or saying something stupid in a really important meeting. Now that you're born, Mommy is yesterday's news. She no longer walks on water and she's finding it hard to cope. She's wondering why all the nice strangers who used to run to her expectant side to open doors for her are always MIA when she's struggling to jam your SUV-sized stroller through the tiny nonautomated Starbucks doorway without spilling half her extra-hot latté on your lap. The world could now care less whether you're a boy or a girl; they just want to know what Mommy's done to make you scream so loudly. Recently, she's even caught herself longing for the unsolicited belly strokes that used to make her recoil. Now she has only your dirty diapers to thank for that.

KNOCKED UP IN A CUP

(nonalcoholic)

INGREDIENTS

5 ounces cranberry juice

1 ounce club soda

Cherry

INSTRUCTIONS

Fill a tall glass with ice. Pour in the cranberry juice
and club soda, and stir. Impregnate with a cherry.

NOTE

Break out your maternity jeggings and a
basketball and enjoy this mocktail for old
times' sake.

HOW BADLY YOU NEED THIS DRINK

ℒ SHE CAN'T TAKE A SICK DAY ℓ

Mommy feels like shit. Mommy wants to turn off all the lights, crawl under the duvet, and die. Before you were born, Mommy could call in sick and *still get paid*. But now that she's on maternity leave, when Mommy feels like she's been run over by a truck she can't even take a minute off, let alone a whole day. She's desperate for even twenty minutes of sleep, but she can't get it because you're teething, or you're constipated, or you're just being an asshole. In between cold sweats, Mommy reaches for her surefire OTC cocktail, SudafedBenylinNyquilTylenol. **WARNING: Nursing mothers are screwed as meds will adversely affect milk supply.** NOOOOooooo. In that moment, Mommy has delusions of getting relief by snorting bath salts. At least she'll get to rest when you take your morning nap. Oh, you've dropped your morning nap today? Awesome. This is Mommy's fault for not getting the free flu shot given to pregnant women when she had the chance.

A SHOT OF JÄGERMEISTER

NOTE

Countries across Europe have been using it as
medicine for years and they always know what
they're doing! (*cough* Greece *cough*)

HOW BADLY YOU NEED THIS DRINK

ꙮ sex ꙮ

Mommy used to love having sex with Daddy. When you eventually ask, "Mommy, where do babies come from?" she will be tempted to respond with the truth: a trip to Agent Provocateur, a remix of Marvin Gaye's "Sexual Healing," and a bottle of red wine. And in the early days of pregnancy, it was still game on, thanks to raging hormones and a growing rack. But CLICHÉ ALERT: Now that she's a Mommy, her sex life has taken a nosedive into nonexistent. She looks at her Track My Sex Life app with dread when she realizes it's been weeks since she put out and Daddy's getting cagey. Even though it looks like Picasso's *Femme en Pleurs* down there, he's still really into doing it. Maybe it's because her boobs are porn-star huge. But if he tries to touch them after you've been gnawing on them all day, she will totally go for it! If the definition of *go for it* is "lose it." On top of which, Mommy hasn't picked up her Venus Embrace razor in three weeks, and her last bikini wax was just before you were born.

AN ORGASM

INGREDIENTS

$1/_3$ ounce Amaretto

$1/_3$ ounce coffee liqueur

$1/_3$ ounce Irish cream

INSTRUCTIONS

Combine all the ingredients in a shaker with ice.
Shake well and strain into a shot glass. Make another
for your partner and enjoy simultaneously. Just like
old times!

HOW BADLY YOU NEED THIS DRINK

LACK OF SLEEP

Some women at Mommy Group complain that their babies are not sleeping through the night. "My Liam wakes up once in a twelve-hour period! We're going to have to hire a night doula." What. The. Fuck. Not only will you not sleep through the night, you're up every two hours. Mommy has been forced to replace actual restorative shut-eye with caffeine and carbs. She was going to max out a college savings plan so you could go to Harvard, but at $10 a pop for a Venti and an artisanal cheese scone, it looks like you'll be going to the First Choice Haircutters Academy. To add insult to injury, after desperately attempting to nurse you to sleep last night, you puked Linda Blair–style down her threadbare Bravado bra. Mommy was too exhausted to do anything about it, so she spent the night in someone else's vomit. Memories of spring break in Cancún. Although being up all night then was by choice. (And awesome.)

MEXICAN COFFEE

INGREDIENTS

5 ounces hot coffee

1 ounce coffee liqueur

½ ounce tequila

INSTRUCTIONS

Pour the coffee in a mug, add the coffee liqueur and tequila, and stir. Enjoy your much-needed caffeine fix hot and steamy, just like that night on the beach with Ernesto. Or was it Todd? Not important. Vacation flings don't count toward your "number."

HOW BADLY YOU NEED THIS DRINK

THE OFFICE VISIT

The time has come for Mommy's mandatory "bring the baby to the office" trip. Mommy carefully scheduled the visit around your nursing schedule, as her lack of skill with the Hooter Hider would inevitably lead to a traumatic nipple-flashing-the-CFO incident. Mommy's in-box has been overflowing with emails about how excited everyone is to meet you, although she knows they're actually just dying to see how much of her baby weight she's lost. None of her business casual wear fits, so Mommy had to truck it to Banana Republic yesterday to buy a half-price polyester dress she'll never wear again and take her MAC Studio Fix out of hiding. Mommy will put on her best "really interested" face as she's updated on the latest office politics and fiscal-year market share progress, while secretly dreaming about the *Downton Abbey* episode on her DVR. As you're passed around from one colleague to the next, she'll also try to block out what she recently read about keyboards being five times germier than toilet seats. Mommy really hopes you don't cry, unless it's when she's caught in conversation with that guy from accounting who can't read social cues.

THE SEVEN-DAY WEEKEND

INGREDIENTS

½ ounce pineapple rum

½ ounce light rum

6 ounces lemon-lime soda

INSTRUCTIONS

Chill a cocktail glass and fill it with ice. Add all the ingredients and stir. Enjoy while celebrating the fact that you can wear pajamas 24/7.

HOW BADLY YOU NEED THIS DRINK

HER HAIR IS FALLING OUT

When Mommy was pregnant, she was basically living in a Pantene commercial with her long, luscious locks. For some wonderful reason, nature offsets swollen ankles and stretch marks with thick, lustrous hair. It was a Rapunzel-fest. But now it's *Meet the Klumps* in her shower drain. She's finding hair everywhere—her clothes, the furniture—and her hairbrush looks like a hamster got caught in it. Today she found a strand wrapped around your pinky finger, cutting off your circulation. Apparently Mommy is losing up to five hundred strands a day. She feels like G.I. Jane's flabby postpartum sister. Remember when Sinead O'Connor shaved off all her hair, then went postal on *Saturday Night Live* and tore up a picture of the pope? Lack of hair can make women go crazy. Maybe Mommy should go to the salon and get a fresh new do with all her massive amounts of free time. HA HA HA HA HA. Mommy's choices now are to just hack it off or buy an array of scrunchies. Mommy's laughing on the outside, but on the inside, those tears are shed as fast as each much-missed strand.

HAIR OF THE DOG

INGREDIENTS

2 ounces gin

Splash of lemon juice

Dash of Tabasco sauce

Slice of chile pepper

INSTRUCTIONS

Combine all the ingredients in a shaker with ice.
Shake well, strain into a glass, and garnish with a
pepper slice. Enjoy with a nice hat.

HOW BADLY YOU NEED THIS DRINK

THE IN-LAWS

When one of Mommy's parents does something that makes her blood boil, at least she can vent freely to Daddy, knowing that he'll always take her side. When Daddy's parents are around, it's a different story. Mommy feels compelled to play the part of perfect mother, doting wife, and competent household manager, not to mention hostess extraordinaire. This would be challenging in the best of times, but it's virtually impossible when Mommy is hormonal and sleep deprived, particularly when Grandma can't help but insert her opinion every five seconds. Though Mommy appreciates that the stove is finally being used, she longs to be passive-aggressive with Daddy, watch back-to-back episodes of *Homeland,* and not have to dress you in a fuzzy bear bodysuit because Grandma is convinced you're on the verge of hypothermia *in July*. Meanwhile, ever since Grandpa accidentally walked in on Mommy breast-feeding, he will no longer make eye contact. With anyone. Sometimes Mommy thinks it'd be easier if Daddy's parents lived on a remote island off the coast of Mozambique, but when you roll over for the first time, Mommy can't wait to Skype them with the news. If only they understood The Internet.

KEEP THE PEACE

INGREDIENTS

1 ounce sloe gin

1 ounce lemon juice

Splash of grenadine

Club soda

INSTRUCTIONS

Chill a cocktail glass. Pour in the gin and lemon juice.
Add the grenadine and top with club soda. Garnish
with an olive branch.

HOW BADLY YOU NEED THIS DRINK

CELEBRITY MOMS

Angelina Jolie. Natalie Portman. Beyoncé. It seems like all of Hollywood can pop out a baby and look effortlessly malnourished the next day. Mariah Carey shit out twins and eight minutes later was the nude spokesmodel for Weight Watchers. Mommy wishes she wasn't still living in her Gap maternity jeans, but unfortunately she doesn't have a personal trainer or a weight-loss-inducing habit like heroin. According to Mommy's number-one online news source, People.com, movie-star matriarchs insist that the secret to losing the pregnancy weight is "carrying around a baby all day!" Mommy knows this is celebrity-speak for bulimia, because no A-lister carries her own child. Plus, Mommy actually does carry you all day and the only thing she has to show for it is a herniated disc. Though Mommy admits she loves that her new double Ds look like they were done by Dr. 90210, she sometimes longs to look glamorously on the brink of death like Too-Posh-to-Push Spice.

RED CARPET FIZZ

INGREDIENTS

3 ounces pink Moët

½ ounce Grand Marnier

½ ounce lime juice

2 ounces orange juice

INSTRUCTIONS

Chill a Champagne flute and fill it with ice. Pour in all the ingredients and gently stir. Enjoy every caloric sip, unlike actual celebrities, who subsist only on air and the perpetual need for validation.

HOW BADLY YOU NEED THIS DRINK

CELEBRITY BABIES

It's not just the coke-thin Hollywood moms that give Mommy a complex. The celebri-tots look just as glam being carried by their nannies and dressed head to toe in Burberry Baby. Mommy shops off-the-rack (the sales rack) at H&M Kids in a futile attempt at Keeping Up with the Kardashi-babies. At least she can take comfort in knowing that those Tiffany silver spoon–fed babies have the worst names ever ("Son, we named you after a paint color") and that their careers will peak on the reality show *My Mom Was a Celebrity and Now I'm in Rehab,* premiering summer 2037. Besides, Mommy is on trend since having a baby is "the hottest accessory of the season" according to *InStyle*. It's just that sometimes she quietly wishes she also had a Birkin bag to tote your diapers in.

THE CELEBRI-TINI

INGREDIENTS

1 ounce light rum

1 ounce coconut liqueur

3 ounces guava juice

Splash of grenadine

INSTRUCTIONS

Fill a glass with ice. Pour in all the ingredients and
stir. Enjoy while finally reading that 2012 issue of
People you found jammed in a drawer. Wait, Poehler
and Arnett broke up? NOOOOoooooooo!

HOW BADLY YOU NEED THIS DRINK

25

‿ LABOR IN THE MOVIES ‿

As Mommy nurses you at 3 AM in front of Lifetime, it occurs to her that every labor scene in every movie ever produced is total bullshit. Real labor lasts for what felt like eight years, but in the movies there's always a mad rush to the hospital and the baby's delivered with only minutes to spare. Also, every birth scene is scripted with the following dialogue:

WIFE: Drugs! Give me the drugs!
HUSBAND: Remember to breathe. Hee hee ho. Hee hee ho.
WIFE: You did this to me, you bastard!

Despite her pleas, it's always "too late" for the epidural. After three pushes that look less challenging than introductory Pilates, out emerges the "newborn," plucked from an Anne Geddes calendar and looking six months old. In the biopic about Mommy's life, she's pretty sure the scene that comes next—where you're screaming and she's sobbing as she attempts to latch you to her throbbing boobs while perched on a bag of frozen peas—will end up on the cutting room floor.

THE BOX OFFICE SMASH

INGREDIENTS

5 fresh strawberries

4 fresh basil leaves

Squeeze of lemon

½ ounce simple syrup

1½ ounces vodka

3 ounces club soda

Wedge of lemon

INSTRUCTIONS

Muddle the strawberries, with green leaves removed, and basil in a mixing glass. Pour in the lemon juice, simple syrup, and vodka. Transfer the mixture to an ice-filled glass and top with club soda. Stir and garnish with a lemon wedge. Pour yourself one just before the scene where the protagonist slips back into her size 0 wardrobe the day after she gives birth.

HOW BADLY YOU NEED THIS DRINK

26

EVERYTHING MAKES HER CRY

Mommy used to have the emotional resolve of Helen Mirren in *The Queen*. Now she cries when she misplaces her Lip Smackers. She's not sure if it's hormones, sleep deprivation, or Beatrix Potter books that have caused this new psychosis, but she's become annoyingly sensitive. The following may have made her cry this week: Being put on hold. The zoo. Socks you've outgrown.

Even the wrong tweet can send her into a tailspin of tears, so she had to unfollow Miley Cyrus. The other thing that can cause her to explode into hysterics is this: absolutely nothing. She's an emotional ticking time bomb and Daddy's in the trenches. If he has any chance of coming out of this alive, he needs to learn the following phrases ASAP: "Cloud White and Decorator White *are* completely different colors," "Let's hire a cleaning lady," and "My mother is being unreasonable."

J.T.'S G & T

INGREDIENTS

1 ounce gin

3 ounces tonic

Splash of grapefruit juice

Zest of lemon

INSTRUCTIONS

Cry me a river of booze by bringing sexy back to an
old classic. Fill a glass with ice. Pour in the gin, tonic,
and grapefruit juice and stir. Garnish with lemon zest
and a box of Kleenex. It's hormonal happy hour!

HOW BADLY YOU NEED THIS DRINK

27

THE DIAPER BAG

Before you were born, Mommy used to splurge on the season's latest handbag. Now she admonishes such extravagant spending and can regularly be found pillaging the sales rack at Old Navy. Her adorable Chanel clutch has been replaced by an oversized Skip Hop messenger tote which, like you, she carries everywhere. What it lacks in style it makes up for in cubic volume, stuffed to the brim with everything from depleted Starbucks cards to Baby Mum-Mum wrappers. Also in tow are a half-dozen backup Onesies in preparation for the diaper explosion that will inevitably happen five minutes after leaving home. At which point Mommy will realize she's down to her very last wipe. Mommy is painfully aware that she's headed down a slippery slope lined with sensible shoes and high-waisted denim, but the stench of your dirty diapers has fried the parts of her brain responsible for pride and personal care.

COCO CHANEL

INGREDIENTS

1 ounce gin

1 ounce coffee liqueur

1 ounce cream

INSTRUCTIONS

Combine all the ingredients in a shaker with cracked ice. Shake well and strain into a crystal martini glass. Take off those mom jeans and remember what Coco said: "A girl should be two things: classy and fabulous" (read: not wearing front pleats).

HOW BADLY YOU NEED THIS DRINK

28

꩜ PUBLIC TRANSPORTATION ꩜

If it wasn't for the fact that Daddy needed the Corolla today, there is no way Mommy would subject you to this underground hell to get to Gymboree. On public transportation, all common decency goes out the emergency glass window. Suddenly people think it's okay to clip their nails, eat a falafel, and hum in public—and that's all done by the *same person*. Not to mention the sweaty man next to you who missed the memo on soap and water as basic tools of life. At least you have more teeth than he does. The tweens at the end of the car are dressed like Nicki Minaj, reek of Marlboros, and are swearing like they're on an HBO special. Mommy silently prays you join the Mathletes. All this stimulation is too much for your tiny brain to process and you won't stop screeching until Mommy picks you up. Even though she's holding an infant while careening through a tunnel at fifty miles per hour, no one offers Mommy a seat, and she refuses to hold the pole because of the 412 strains of bacteria it's harboring. "The next station is Nervous Breakdown." Despite the fact that Mommy is struggling to push the Bugaboo with one hand while holding you and your diaper bag with the other, no one clears a path as she tries to get off. Mommy manages to claw through the throngs of people like Moses parting the Red Sea only to discover this station doesn't have a working elevator. Thud thud thud. Mommy drags you up 478 stairs and gives you mild whiplash while no one offers to help. Slow clap for humanity.

OFF THE RAILS

INGREDIENTS

1 ounce of rye, rum, vodka, or gin

4 ounces fruit punch

INSTRUCTIONS

Fill a glass with ice. Pour in your bar rail of choice
and fruit punch, and stir. Unlike the guy sitting next
to you, don't consume out of a paper bag.

HOW BADLY YOU NEED THIS DRINK

EXPLOSIVE POO

Mommy used to get shit done. Now she gets shit on. How does such a tiny person consistently produce so much volume? It gets in every little crevice down there. It goes up your back. It goes down your legs. It goes sideways? First it started out as sticky black tar. Then the mustard stuff. Which, in hindsight, wasn't so bad. Mommy didn't realize how good she had it when you were exclusively fed breast milk. Now that you're eating solids, this shit is getting real, fast. The inaccurately named Diaper Genie isn't very magical at all because the smell permeates the whole house. Unless, at the drop point, someone (read: Daddy) quickly runs the hot mess to the green bin outside. There's no waiting for Daddy to get home though, as The Situation must be dealt with immediately lest you get a diaper rash. But oh, the horror that unfolds with the diaper. No one accurately prepared Mommy for this, and there are some triple-poo days when she actually throws up in her mouth a little. Of course, Mommy tries to remain calm, even when you drop a deuce in the bath, or in the Jolly Jumper, or on the wall, or OH MY GOD WHAT IS THAT IN MOMMY'S HAIR? Shit.

A MUDSLIDE

INGREDIENTS

Chocolate syrup

½ ounce vodka

½ ounce coffee liqueur

½ ounce Irish cream

Splash of milk

INSTRUCTIONS

Drizzle chocolate syrup around the inside rim of a glass, and then fill the glass with ice. Pour in the vodka, coffee liqueur, Irish cream, and milk and stir.

HOW BADLY YOU NEED THIS DRINK

YOU'RE SICK

Sometimes your explosive poo becomes even more explosive. This means you're sick. Even though Mommy struggles to remember a two-week stretch in your existence where you *weren't* exhibiting some symptom of illness, seeing that first trickle of green snot oozing from your nose still sends her into a tailspin of hysteria. Cue obsessive WebMD surfing and an exponential increase in the number of orders barked at Daddy. The Internet is never wrong, so she confirms that you have West Nile Virus. After a four-hour trip to the emergency room, it turns out it's just a common cold. Now Mommy is faced with the moral dilemma of whether to quarantine you at the expense of her sanity or drag you and your germs to music class, where you'll undoubtedly lick multiple tambourines and shove your snot-drenched finger into any open infant mouth within reach. Mommy chooses the latter, armed with a story involving allergy season if challenged.

THE FLØRENCE NIGHTIN-ALE

INGREDIENTS

1 bottle cold ale

Shot of tomato juice

INSTRUCTIONS

Pour the ale and tomato juice into a pint-sized glass.
Chase with echinacea.

NOTE

Cheers to your health (while you can, because
guess what? You're catching that cold
tomorrow).

HOW BADLY YOU NEED THIS DRINK

MOMMY BRAIN

Mommy Brain: noun \'mä-mē \'brān\. A phenomenon whereby a mother's previously sophisticated cognitive capacity rapidly diminishes to that of an ousted *Bachelor* contestant. Fueled by chronic sleep deprivation, overexposure to *The Very Hungry Caterpillar,* and speaking exclusively in nonsense syllables and baby talk, the condition is characterized by the sufferer's inability to perform previously routine tasks such as matching a skirt and top, finding her phone in her purse, and reading anything other than PerezHilton. com without needing to consult her Dictionary app. The condition can be reversed, in theory, when the sufferer's offspring embarks on fourth-grade math and she is forced to figure out what the fuck long division is all over again.

THE BRAIN FREEZE

INGREDIENTS

Blue curaçao

Sugar

¾ ounce Amaretto

¾ ounce melon liqueur

INSTRUCTIONS

Chill a glass. Rim it with blue curaçao and then sugar.
Fill the glass with crushed ice, pour in the Amaretto
and melon liqueur, and stir. Serve with a blank stare.

HOW BADLY YOU NEED THIS DRINK

 BABY GAP

Mommy has never spent more time at the mall than she has while on maternity leave. The spacious family washrooms, climate-controlled promenades, and stroller-friendly food court make it Disneyland for Maternity Mommies. The irony of this is that Mommy has never been more broke; however, she can't resist falling into Baby Gap. Price check: This miniature pair of skinny jeans costs more than the pair Mommy's wearing. Mommy's maternity-leave benefits barely cover a Mega Mango Jamba Juice, but Visa will cover this argyle sweater vest with skull-and-crossbones embroidery. A bear riding a motorcycle? On a Onesie? Clearly you need to own this. (Sociopolitical pause: Mommy really hopes that these clothes weren't made by children not much older than you.) Oooh, little shoes! Mommy will buy several pairs, because you can't walk yet, so that makes perfect sense. Mommy's closet looks like the "before" segment on *Extreme Makeover,* but your wardrobe could be a photo essay in *Vogue.*

THE SHOPPING MAUL

INGREDIENTS

½ ounce cherry brandy

½ ounce light rum

½ ounce dark rum

3 ounces grapefruit juice

1 ounce orange juice

Splash of grenadine

INSTRUCTIONS

Before you look at this month's Visa bill, make
yourself one of these. Fill a glass with crushed ice.
Pour in all the ingredients and stir.

HOW BADLY YOU NEED THIS DRINK

PLASTIC TOYS

Mommy-to-be was all holier than thou with her "We will only buy nontoxic, eco-friendly wooden toys handcrafted by Amish people" declarations, made while sipping her organic soy chai. Cut to now. Mommy's house looks like Fisher-Price puked its entire catalog all over her ten-by-twelve-foot living room floor, and now that you're old enough to have an opinion, you couldn't be less interested in the wooden duck on a string, which is now collecting dust in the corner. Mommy can run, but she definitely can't hide from the rainbow-colored explosion of plastic toys from China that's invaded every corner of her home. P.S., Mommy can't even run, thanks to impaling herself on a rogue LEGO piece yesterday, an experience only slightly less painful than labor. Besides worrying about the long-term effects of the polyurethane you're ingesting (refer to Exhibit A—the plastic sheep ear she recently found nestled in your dirty diaper), Mommy is too embarrassed by her hypocrisy to invite anyone over for playdates anymore. And leaving the house to socialize is too overwhelming thanks to the chronic headache she's developed from all the off-gassing.

CHINA WHITE

INGREDIENTS

½ ounce white crème de cacao

½ ounce vodka

½ ounce Irish cream

Dash of cinnamon

INSTRUCTIONS

Combine the crème de cacao, vodka, and Irish cream
in a shaker with ice. Shake well and strain into an
ice-filled glass. Top with cinnamon.

HOW BADLY YOU NEED THIS DRINK

MOMMY AND ME YOGA

Mommy used to kill it when it came to cardio. She could spin for an hour and still look adorable enough to flirt with Braedon, the twenty-six-year-old trainer/man candy. The gym was a social place and Mommy was on the A-list—that *A* stood for "ass," and hers was tight. Now Mommy does baby yoga. This is not a workout but an excuse to drop $20 to do one Downward-Facing Dog and spend the other forty-three minutes in a Circle Bitch about sleep training. Mommy is still hypercompetitive, only now it's over whose baby is doing what first. Mommy has actually pushed you to do things you're not ready for, like propping you up to sitting, then feigned surprise when you promptly toppled over and bashed your head on a yoga block. The four calories burned trying to keep the snot-covered communal toys out of your mouth during class are made up for in spades by the post-Namaste trip to the Fair Trade coffee shop, where a carob-chip spelt cookie packs a whopping seventeen grams of fat. Mommy may now live in her Lulus, but she has a feeling the rear view isn't the same.

THE SKINNY BITCH

(Remember when you used to be one?)

INGREDIENTS

5 ounces Diet Coke

1 ounce vodka

Squeeze of lime

INSTRUCTIONS

Fill a glass with ice. Pour in all the ingredients and
stir. Only fifty-six calories!

HOW BADLY YOU NEED THIS DRINK

35

SLEEP TRAINING

It's not even 10 AM and you've been screaming in your crib for what feels like an eternity. Actually it's been four minutes. The longest four minutes of Mommy's life. All she wants to do is run upstairs and sweep you up into her arms, but Dr. Ferber says to let you cry for up to an hour. An hour? Mommy can't take it. She's tried everything from all the Guaranteed to Work books: *The No-Cry Sleep Solution; Healthy Sleep Habits, Happy Child; The Sleepeasy Solution.* All have been epic failures. The only thing that used to work was pushing you around and around the same streets in your stroller. The bonus to that was the baby weight melted off as Mommy walked for hours a day. The best Bugaboo accessory purchase to date has been the cup holder, as Mommy mapped out her route based on Starbucks locations. Now that you're older and more alert, this trick no longer works because you're distracted by every dog, car, or light gust of wind. Depriving you of naps is "akin to torture," the books say, so you have to stay in your crib and cry it out, or throw up, or both. If it's any consolation, Mommy is also crying it out. She really wishes she could numb the sinking feeling that she's The Worst Mother in the World. Plus, it's hard to hear *The View* over all the combined sobbing.

THE SELF-RESTRAINT

(nonalcoholic)

INGREDIENTS

2 ounces orange juice

2 ounces pineapple juice

2 ounces pomegranate juice

1 ounce grenadine

½ ounce almond syrup

Fresh mint leaves

Pineapple spear

INSTRUCTIONS

Chill a tall glass. Combine the orange, pineapple, and
pomegranate juices, grenadine, and almond syrup in
a blender with cracked ice and blend until smooth.
Pour into the glass, garnish with the mint and
pineapple spear, and turn up the volume.

HOW BADLY YOU NEED THIS DRINK

THE FAMILY PET

Before you were born, Sparky was the center of Mommy and Daddy's universe. Sparky was the Test Baby and was spoiled as such with free-range bison meat, monogrammed dishes, and endless affection. Sparky had a Facebook page with funny status updates like "Chasing tail tonight, look out ladies" and "It's Thursday? Feels like Friday." Now poor Sparky is *pet-sona non grata*. This has led to some bad behavior, including chewing all your baby toys and Mommy's entire collection of Aldo shoes. Never mind the fact that Sparky completely failed as the Test Baby. It turns out Mommy and Daddy can't just leave you for a night by turning on the National Geographic channel and putting out a bowl of kibble. Speaking of kibble, yesterday Mommy caught you eating some off the kitchen floor. You won't eat homemade, wholesome food, but you will eat dehydrated cow testicles or whatever else is in pet chow. Not only is the entire IKEA EKTORP sofa either clawed or covered in spit-up, but it seems both you and Sparky are in a literal pissing contest to mark your territory. These days, Mommy's always cleaning up someone else's pee: yours, Sparky's, *and Daddy's*. Maybe when you grow up, you'll have better aim.

A SALTY DOG

INGREDIENTS

Lemon juice

Salt

1 ounce vodka

3 ounces grapefruit juice

INSTRUCTIONS

Rim a glass with lemon juice and then salt. Fill the glass with ice. Pour in the vodka and grapefruit juice, and stir. Serve on a short leash.

HOW BADLY YOU NEED THIS DRINK

EX-BOYFRIENDS

Sometimes, when she's covered in baby barf, tortured by sleep deprivation, and as hormonal as ~~Chastity~~ Chaz Bono, Mommy fantasizes about What Could Have Been. This involves mentally scrolling through (and, real talk, Facebook creeping) her roster of exes. Here's what plays out during her *It's a Wonderful Life* flashback of relationships past:

The Big Man with a Small Penis: Would have made her a kept woman, complete with a mansion, four nannies plus a night nurse, and a barely legal mistress.

The Nice Guy with No Backbone: Would have done whatever she wanted all the time (including every diaper change and late-night feeding!) except go away and/or stop crying.

Questionably Gay Metrosexual Man: Would have done all the cooking, shopping, and cleaning of their adopted child, and Mommy would have become best friends with the massage feature on her showerhead.

The Hot Guy with No Career: Would have motivated Mommy to keep up her Brazilian waxes and lose the baby weight in sexercise while she went broke funding his T-shirt–printing business.

Ultimately, though, when you wrap your pudgy arms around her neck and bare your big toothy grin, Mommy is incredibly grateful for Daddy. They made you together. Then she reminds herself that exes are called exes for a reason.

THE GHOSTS OF
BOYFRIENDS PAST

INGREDIENTS

1 ounce pear nectar

1 ounce cranberry juice

Prosecco

INSTRUCTIONS

Chill a Champagne flute. Pour in the pear nectar and
cranberry juice, and top with Prosecco. Spill a little
on the ground in memory, and close the door (and
your laptop, you stalker!) on the past.

HOW BADLY YOU NEED THIS DRINK

THE WEATHER

Like Mommy's mother-in-law, Mother Nature can be irritating. However, Mommy is going stir-crazy and needs to get you out of the house before you Jackson Pollock another wall. The Weather Channel is as random as her iTunes shuffle, so here's what could play out:

Baby, it's cold outside. Mommy has to wrestle you into multiple layers, including an embarrassing reindeer sweater and a bunting bag worthy of a trek to base camp. You won't wear mittens and you continually throw off your hat. An old lady gives Mommy the stink eye and judges her parenting in another language.

Blame it on the rain. This means Mommy can't walk you anywhere unless she MacGyvers a tent over the stroller. She can't carry an umbrella while pushing your SUV, so Mommy gets soaked. Your hat falls into your eyes, rendering you temporarily blind, but Mommy can't adjust it because of the Fortress of Waterproof Solitude surrounding you.

Feelin' hot, hot, hot. You're too little to wear sunscreen, so you have to wear a UV-blocking Hazmat suit, leaving you sweaty and pissed off. You refuse to wear your junior Ray-Bans and keep ripping off your ironic straw fedora. The hat goes MIA. Even though you and Mommy were almost home, she has to retrace her steps to find it. She sees your hat in the middle of the road. The hat gets run over by a Range Rover. You laugh and laugh. Mommy should be frustrated that yet another $22 has been flushed down the proverbial Diaper Genie, but instead she silently applauds your sociopolitical stance on hipsters and makes a mental note that your style is more Hugo Boss than Unemployed Musician.

A HURRYCANE

INGREDIENTS

1 ounce dark rum

2 ounces lemon juice

2 ounces passion fruit syrup

Slices of orange

Cherry

INSTRUCTIONS

Hurry and combine the dark rum, lemon juice, and passion fruit syrup in a shaker with ice. Shake well and strain into an ice-filled hurricane glass (it's tulip shaped, but really, any glass will do). Garnish with the orange slices and cherry.

HOW BADLY YOU NEED THIS DRINK

39

TV

Mommy's weekly TV consumption has skyrocketed since your birth, rivaling levels seen only in the early 1990s, when she was a latchkey kid. At least back then her female TV role models were Angela Bower and Clair Huxtable. Now she's stuck with Khloé Kardashian. The first spike occurred in your early weeks, when Mommy's maternity-leave routine consisted of parking herself in front of the (appropriately named) boob tube every two hours while you suckled on her breast for marathon feeding sessions. After a decade of resorting to Soapcentral.com for updates, finally she could watch the drama unfold in real time, a perk that helped her cope with the tragic loss of her income and abs that accompanied your birth. Unfortunately, this period was short-lived, as Mommy's daytime routine soon evolved to that of an Ironman athlete between cross-city treks to Gymboree and wrestling competitions with high chairs and strollers. Mommy's days have become so physically taxing that by the time your bedtime rolls around, collapsing in front of the TV is the only activity that doesn't leave her breathless. Sometimes Mommy wishes it was still PC to park you in front of *Sesame Street,* so she could (learn to) cook a meal or read something other than the What to Expect series, safe in the knowledge that Big Bird's alphabet song was permeating your subconscious mind. But the interweb is abuzz with warnings that TV before the age of two will supposedly saddle you with attention-deficit disorder for life. Even though she knows that next year a new study will be released showing Einstein-like brain patterns in kids exposed to *Dora the Explorer* from birth, in yet another victory for Mommy Guilt, the remote control has been relegated to a teething device in your presence.

THE BRAIN COCKTAIL

INGREDIENTS

1 ounce peach schnapps

1 ounce Irish cream

1 dash grenadine

INSTRUCTIONS

Pour the schnapps into a highball glass. Add the Irish cream to the center and top with grenadine. Serve with a TV dinner.

HOW BADLY YOU NEED THIS DRINK

40

FACEBOOK

Pre-baby Facebook was fun. Post-baby Facebook is hell. The status updates from the non-baby crew are: Exotic travel! References to music! Checked in at hipster pizzeria slash tequila bar! Mommy longs for the days where she was part of that elite crew who put their night back together through tagged photos and Foursquare. And what the hell is a meme? Mommy can't keep up.

The status updates from the baby crew are: My baby! Don't you love my profile pic that's of my baby? Check out another upload of my baby! Below the photo there are comments from other parents about how cute the baby is, followed by many exclamation points. Mommy only wishes she could post what everyone's really thinking: That kid ain't right. Hey look, Mommy has a friend request! Sadly, it's Insert Baby Name Here's Mom from playgroup. (Ignore.) After commenting on a link to the latest OK Go video in an effort to project an image that she's still cool, Mommy was tagged covered in regurgitated rice cereal at Salsa Babies Dance Class. Mommy's status update: Feeling as relevant as Myspace. (Wait, three friends "like" this?)

THE FRIEND REQUEST

INGREDIENTS

5 ounces sparkling wine

1 ounce raspberry vodka

Splash of Chambord

Fresh raspberries

INSTRUCTIONS

Pour the wine, vodka, and Chambord into a
Champagne flute and stir. Garnish with raspberries
and enjoy the instant friends you make when you
serve it.

HOW BADLY YOU NEED THIS DRINK

41

~~~ GLØBAL WARMING ~~~

According to her old Match.com profile, Mommy has always cared about the environment. Though she recycles her Diet Coke cans and avoids eating things like baby panda frittata, she may have *slightly* exaggerated when she said her perfect date night was "hand washing the poor baby penguins from the Dawn commercials." The thing is, buying a car that runs on sunshine and hugs just wasn't high on her list of priorities. Since you've been born, however, she is struck by just how shitty we've been treating our planet. It's a real buzzkill to actually watch the YouTube video of Gordon Ramsay's shark fin soup exposé or discover via Twitter that the ozone is so screwed that soon we're all going to look like the cast of *Jersey Shore*. If the North Pole melts and all of Santa's reindeer drown in a flash flood, she's pretty sure that will ruin your childhood. When Mommy really thinks about it, she worries not only about the future of our planet but about the growing threat of violence, poverty, and disease, and how she'll ever protect you from all of it. (Whoa, that shit got real.) No longer can Mommy turn a blind eye to *Mother Earth: Special Victims Unit*. However, Mommy draws the eco-line at cloth diapers. After the Exxon disaster that came out of you this morning, she's going to have to stick with disposable.

ORGANIC LOCAL WINE

NOTE

Feel great about your headache the next day.
The more throbbing it is, the more you did your
part for the environment.

HOW BADLY YOU NEED THIS DRINK

42

SWIM CLASS

Mommy was punch drunk from labor when she signed you up for Infant Swim at the local public pool. She had visions of you floating peacefully in the water, an extension of the womb, but failed to consider this would mean pouring herself into postpartum swimwear. Visual reference: sausage bursting on a BBQ. All Mommy owns are neon string bikinis from a previous life, but she can't bear to buy a sensible one piece from the I've Given Up line at Sears. As a small (large) bonus, her boobs have swollen to the size of Jessica Simpson's and have never looked trashier, in a good way. She's hoping this distracts from the train wreck happening south of the double-D border, cruelly highlighted by a now-permanent *linea nigra*. The class is only twenty minutes long, but it takes almost an hour to wriggle you into swim diapers and get herself dressed while balancing you on a germ-infested bench. One round of the "Fishy Wishy" song and your lips have turned blue, so Mommy wraps you in a towel and lets her dream that you'll become the next Missy "the Missile" Franklin float away with the pool noodle. As she dries you off while plodding back down the pool deck, Mommy can already feel the plantar wart growing on her foot. At no point during this experience did you look like the baby on the cover of the Nirvana album. Oh well, whatever, nevermind.

THE PØØL PARTY

INGREDIENTS

1 ounce blue curaçao

3 ounces lemonade

Splash of lemon-lime soda

INSTRUCTIONS

Fill a glass with ice. Pour in the curaçao, lemonade,
and lemon-lime soda and stir.

NOTE

Smells like teen spirits.

HOW BADLY YOU NEED THIS DRINK

FLYING

When Mommy learned that babies fly free until they're two (at which point they're charged the *full fare*!), she decided it was time to rack up some serious air miles, even if that meant the occasional solo mission without her wingman, Daddy. Cut to your very first flight. When Mommy was single, she remembers seeing a parent with child in tow and praying that person wouldn't sit next to her. Now she *is* that person. Mommy has changed two dirty diapers, flashed half of economy class, and endured five judgmental stares, and the captain hasn't even turned on the FASTEN SEAT BELT sign yet. Meanwhile, Mommy might as well have bought you a full-price fare with all the extra charges she's incurred for carting the following across the country: your Pack 'n Play, car seat, stroller, wardrobe, and the hundred diapers you'll blow through by Thursday. It takes an excruciating hour of pacing up and down the aisle, but Mommy finally manages to rock you to sleep. Only for you to wake up twenty minutes later, at which point she's barely made it past the opening credits of the in-flight movie. Unfortunately, the only thing entertaining you at the moment is licking the fold-down tray and ingesting pieces of the tattered *Sky-Mall* magazine. The way this trip is going, she will barely be able to summon up the courage to board the return flight home, let alone take advantage of JetBlue's seat sale for trip number two. Looks like Mommy can tuck her passport away in the place she keeps sleep, downtime, and white clothing, only to be unpacked once you're old enough for overnight camp.

THE AVIATOR

INGREDIENTS

1 ounce gin

¼ ounce maraschino liqueur

¼ ounce apricot brandy

Splash of lemon juice

INSTRUCTIONS

Combine all the ingredients in a shaker with ice.
Shake well and strain into a glass.

NOTE

Airsick bag optional.

HOW BADLY YOU NEED THIS DRINK

44

___ REAL ESTATE ___

Mommy and Daddy used to look for property based on number of exposed beams and proximity to independent espresso bars. Now it's based solely on school district and parks per square mile. They had to sell their fantastic downtown sub-penthouse loft with concrete floors and angles and have traded it in for a tiny, leaky money pit with a yard covered in weeds in a family-friendly neighborhood. Mommy loved making no effort whatsoever to know her neighbors and avoiding eye contact in the elevator. Now she has to memorize everyone's name (which involves Post-its lining the inside of her kitchen cabinetry) and force a smile the minute she turns down her tree-lined street. As a general rule, Mommy hates all of humanity—especially when she is this sleep deprived—so this is a daily challenge. No longer can she stumble out of her building and find herself in a trendy restaurant or designer boutique. Now she finds herself wrestling you in and out of the Peg Perego to schlep you to Home Depot. As a small bonus, watching Daddy swear at the lawn mower is kind of Ward Cleaver sexy.

THE WELCOME MAT

INGREDIENTS

1 ounce Pimms

3 ounces lemonade

Splash of ginger ale

Sprig of fresh rosemary

INSTRUCTIONS

Fill a glass with ice. Pour in the Pimms, lemonade, and ginger ale and stir. Garnish with the rosemary from your herb garden. Yes, you have an herb garden now. Invite the neighbors over, slap on an apron, and surrender to your new domestic life.

HOW BADLY YOU NEED THIS DRINK

45

SHE'S ASYMMETRICAL

One day in biology class you'll learn that animals are attracted to other animals who display good symmetry (which the brain apparently equates with good genes and the production of healthy offspring). What's not taught in school is how the story ends: male courts female, they reproduce, and the female is robbed of the very thing that attracted her mate in the first place.

Exhibit A: Mommy's *rack*. The wonders of uneven milk supply mean sometimes Mommy's right breast is a glorious double D, while her lowly left could play peek-a-boob under a Hershey's Kisses wrapper.

Exhibit B: Mommy's *arms*. From holding you exclusively on one side since you emerged from the womb, Mommy's left biceps could grace the cover of *MuscleMag* while her right would lose to an Olsen twin in an arm wrestle.

Exhibit C: Mommy's *insides*. She obviously missed the part in *What to Expect* where it explained that your organs shift during pregnancy and then "more or less" go back to their original pre-pregnancy positions. Probably because she was still recovering from the trauma of reading the chapter titled "Stretch Marks, Spider Veins, and the Mask of Pregnancy."

Good thing Daddy is attracted to Mommy for more than her looks. Like the sunny disposition that greets him when he comes home from work fifteen minutes late. Oh, wait.

THE SIDESWIPE

INGREDIENTS

1 ounce vodka

½ ounce cranberry vodka

½ ounce dry vermouth

Fresh strawberry

Peel of lemon

INSTRUCTIONS

Chill a cocktail glass. Combine the vodkas and
vermouth in a shaker with ice. Shake well and
strain into the glass. Garnish with a strawberry and
lemon peel.

NOTE

Best consumed while avoiding mirrors.

HOW BADLY YOU NEED THIS DRINK

46

THE GRØWTH SPURT

The wonderful thing about spending $22 on a pair of baby chinos is that you outgrow them before you and Mommy even leave the mall. The only thing growing faster than you is the mountain of outgrown Onesies causing a fire hazard in the basement. She can't give them away in case she has a second, even though *One and Done* is the Dr. Seuss book Mommy is considering ghostwriting. In an effort to pull back on trips to Carter's, Mommy has been cramming you into clothes that no longer fit, just like Christina Aguilera. At the rate you're growing, you'll soon be wearing Daddy's clothes. (Mommy hopes late-century modern becomes a fashion trend ASAP because Daddy's closet is the wardrobe that time forgot and includes every striped button-down sold at The Gap in the 1990s.) Your growth spurts are giving you major mood swings and you no longer sleep through the night, but Mommy is happy you're growing and healthy—plus you look rad in that oversized paisley sweater vest. For the next five minutes.

A TALL DRINK OF WATER

NOTE

Add vodka.

HOW BADLY YOU NEED THIS DRINK

47

THE BABYSITTER

Mommy can't believe she's going to pay a teenager $40 to sit in her living room for three hours (texting her boyfriend and eating Mommy's cappuccino frozen yogurt directly from the tub) while you lie sleeping in your crib upstairs *the entire time.* But Mommy and Daddy figured that to avoid becoming a statistic, they should spend the occasional Saturday night doing something other than eating take-out Thai food in front of her *Sex and the City* box set, only to doze off before the closing credits. Dressed in her standby LBD and rocking her volumizing mascara, Mommy's actually feeling pretty hot, until the sitter with Brooklyn Decker legs sprouting from a skirt the size of a Bella Band greets her at the front door. At least Mommy gets to enjoy a fancy dinner at the trendy new Italian eatery across town that the single crew keeps checking into on Facebook. Until she does the mental math on the evening's expenses and realizes that this mushroom risotto that she could "totally make at home" (just kidding) is costing her $18 per mouthful. Making conversation is challenging when Mommy and Daddy are both sleep deprived and checking their phones every two minutes to make sure you haven't catapulted out of your crib or started a fire. And downing a bottle of red wine isn't an option when someone has to drive the babysitter home at the end of the night to avoid blowing another $20 on cab fare. If this is the price tag on a night out, Mommy and Daddy are going to have to crack some serious social whip. No more Jennifer Aniston movies or double dates with B-list couples until your thirteenth birthday.

A $12 BOTTLE OF MERLOT AND A PIZZA DELIVERY MENU

NOTE

Sometimes it pays to be boring.

HOW BADLY YOU NEED THIS DRINK

48

DIAPERS

One day, when you ask her why you ended up at community college instead of an Ivy League, Mommy will tell you the tragic story of the evil, vile-smelling villain that made off with your entire education fund: The Diaper. Although your career options are now limited to small-engine repair and dental office administration, at least you have this rad Learn n' Fun pelican sorter that Mommy scored from the Pampers points program. If you think this is traumatic for you, just imagine poor Mommy having to deal with the toxic waste that started coming out of you once she introduced solids to your diet. Good thing Mommy has successfully used labor as leverage to get Daddy to own a disproportionate share of diaper changes, adding to his previous household duties of killing bugs and filling the barbecue with propane. Though the thought of spending more than a grand on diapers in your first year alone is more nauseating than constantly changing them, apparently it's better than what lies ahead when it's time for potty training! (Fodder for *Reasons Mommy Drinks 2*?)

LUXURY LIBATION

INGREDIENTS

3 fresh raspberries

3 fresh blueberries

Cognac

Chilled Champagne

INSTRUCTIONS

Soak the berries in the Cognac for 1 hour. Chill a
Champagne flute. Place the berries in the flute and
top with Champagne.

NOTE

Pamper yourself for a change with this
extravagant cocktail.

HOW BADLY YOU NEED THIS DRINK

NAP TIME

Nap time is the most wonderful time in Mommy's day. In theory. According to her Mommy groups, you are the only baby in the universe not taking two perfect one-hour naps a day. Some days Mommy is lucky if you fall asleep for ten minutes in her arms after forty-five minutes of bouncing you on her former exercise ball (at least it's getting some sort of use). On the mornings when you do magically drift off to sleep in your crib, it's a race against time. The clock tick-tocks down as Jack Bauer echoes in her head: "There's no time!" Mommy has less than sixty minutes to do the following things: make coffee, tackle the laundry Matterhorn, clean applesauce off the kitchen ceiling, stuff a Toaster Strudel in her mouth, make more coffee, throw out the rotting vegetables in her fridge, dry-heave while cleaning out the Diaper Genie, not learn Spanish, and sit down for three minutes of hour four of *The Today Show,* at which point she finally gets why Hoda and Kathie Lee are drinking wine before noon. Mommy thinks it's hysterical that there are Pinterest boards about the crafts and elaborate meals that can be prepared during nap time. Not only is Mommy a prisoner of your schedule, but God forbid you should fall asleep in the car seat before she makes it home, because it will completely screw up your nap and screw Mommy out of the one precious hour she has to accomplish everything. "Sleep when the baby sleeps" chirps every book about the first year. *Yeah right.*

NAP THYME

INGREDIENTS

Lemon juice

Sugar

1 ounce gin

3 ounces club soda

Sprig of fresh thyme

INSTRUCTIONS

Rim a glass with lemon juice and then sugar. Fill the glass with ice. Pour in the gin, club soda, a splash of lemon juice, and sugar to taste. Stir gently. Garnish with the thyme.

HOW BADLY YOU NEED THIS DRINK

50

HOTELS

Nothing says baby-friendly like a two-hundred-square-foot room furnished in glass and teeming with germs. Yet somehow tagging along on Daddy's business trip seemed less overwhelming than coping with single-parent duty back home. So for the next seventy-two hours, you and Mommy are living it up, Dylan McKay–style. Despite her best intentions and a family-sized pack of antibacterial wipes, Mommy's germ-busting mission goes belly up when you beat her to the (shudder) remote control. At least she manages to successfully cram your perishable food supply into the refrigerated section of the minibar, which, if the limp Snickers bar is any indication, is probably set somewhere between room temperature and Calcutta. Mommy can forget about ordering room service and watching HBO while Daddy hits the town with his colleagues. The crib won't fit in the bathroom, so it's lights out at 7 PM thanks to the two inches separating you from the TV. Once she finally manages to soothe you to sleep, Mommy's options for in-room entertainment are limited to holing up in the bathroom with the hotel magazine or Facebook-stalking her former coworkers under her duvet. At least she won't be lying when she updates her status with "Having an amazzzing time in NYC."

MINIBAR MOCKTINI

(nonalcoholic)

INGREDIENTS

Varies depending on minibar contents

INSTRUCTIONS

Fill a glass with ice. Pour equal parts cranberry juice
and pineapple or orange juice and top with a splash
of ginger ale. Enjoy with a pack of $15 cashews; this
one's on Daddy's expense account.

HOW BADLY YOU NEED THIS DRINK

51

THE LAUNDRY

Mommy does laundry all day, every day. Apparently, a clean One-sie is a tractor beam for all things stain-y. The perpetual spin cycle is running up her water bill and has probably killed several baby seals. First it was nuclear newborn poo causing the never-ending fluff 'n' fold. Lately, it's self-feeding. Mommy is worried you're not getting enough nutrients because entire avocados are being mashed into your khakis. Of course, you think this is hilarious. As a prop comic, your go-to routine involves covering yourself in tomato sauce, berries, and squash puree, and the punch line is flinging all of it on to Mommy's one decent H&M wrap dress. Not wanting to risk the slightest chance of light irritation on your tender skin (MOMMY GUILT ALERT), she is only using fragrance-free, chemical-free, function-free detergents, which means no stain comes out ever. She's tempted to dress you all in black and start a Goth Baby trend. Anarchy in the crib!

ANYTHING SUDSY WITH A CLEAN FINISH

HOW BADLY YOU NEED THIS DRINK

52

HOME RENOVATIONS

There's no better time to tackle a major home repair than when you have an infant, said no one ever. Mommy and Daddy learned this the hard way recently when the roof sprung a leak. Mommy is overcome with guilt when she splurges on a Starbucks flavor shot, so plunging thousands of dollars into unplanned debt to repair the water damage and reshingle the roof is giving her angina. Especially with the added challenge of ensuring your safety while living in a wrecking zone. Mommy used to go to painstaking lengths to ensure your every waking hour was filled with the perfect combination of playtime, stimulation, and rest. These days she declares victory if you make it through the day without swallowing a rusty nail or falling through a missing floorboard. And getting you to nap for longer than ten-minute intervals has become impossible now that your sleep sound track of waves and seagulls has been remixed with power saws. After material delays and Disappearing Contractor Syndrome stretch a three-week project to eight, Mommy can at least seek solace that you have a roof over your head and a warm, dry place to play. And then the basement floods.

SCREWDRIVER

INGREDIENTS

1 ounce vodka

6 ounces orange juice

INSTRUCTIONS

Fill a glass with ice. Pour in the vodka, top with the
orange juice, and stir.

NOTE

Helps wash down the permanent layer of
sawdust that covers your home.

HOW BADLY YOU NEED THIS DRINK

THE END OF MATERNITY LEAVE

The time has come for Mommy to head back to work. Going to a place where people listen to her ideas, she is compensated financially for her efforts, and she can enjoy a coffee without it going cold first because someone peed on her is, incredibly, filled with mixed emotion. When people ask her how she's "handling the guilt" of leaving you, she transforms into a Claire Danes meme as her face contorts into that of a screwed-up sad person. As she squats in the supply room pumping milk next to extra pens and industrial-grade Windex, she misses you like crazy (and misses midday naps, track pants, and not trying), but she feels proud to support her family in a job she genuinely loves. No one asks Daddy how he handles the guilt. They only ask him when he has to "babysit." There are some Mommies who quit thriving careers with expense accounts and super-elite frequent-flyer status to be stay-at-home Moms. These women are bat-shit crazy! Or they're saints. Staying at home is *hard*. Then again, balancing motherhood and a career means that no matter where you are, you should be somewhere else. Uh-oh. Here comes the Cry Face again. Damn you, Danes!

A ZOMBIE

(Juggling 3 AM feedings and 7 AM conference
calls will make you feel like one.)

INGREDIENTS

½ ounce dark rum

½ ounce cherry brandy

½ ounce light rum

3 ounces orange juice

1 ounce lemon juice

Dash of grenadine

INSTRUCTIONS

Combine all the ingredients in a shaker with ice.
Shake well and strain into a glass after a long day of
Trying to Be Awesome at Everything.

HOW BADLY YOU NEED THIS DRINK

THE PUMP

Mommy has a love-hate relationship with the pump. Like Mel Gibson in *Braveheart,* it provides "FREEEEEEDOM!" However, Mommy could not feel more like a dairy cow, and not just because she is wearing a cow-printed Slanket. Mommy also doesn't understand how science works because one side explodes while the other barely yields a drop. Mommy thought Daddy would never want to have sex again once he saw her nipples being stretched out into deformed pencil erasers, but Daddy just drowns out the "wig wom wig woms" by turning up *Storage Wars*.

But pumping at home is nothing compared to pumping at the office. There's no faster way *not* to climb the corporate ladder than being walked in on by Mommy's male VP while her boobs are hooked up to the Medela Pump In Style Advanced. It doesn't matter how amazing her quarterly results are. The dude will never forget that moment, and Mommy now needs to update her LinkedIn profile. But pumping is worth it. Even though it can take a full twenty minutes of creeping her frenemies on Facebook to squeeze out five ounces, pumping means she can go back to work and still breast-feed you. It also means she can have a drink. So Mommy will continue to make like The Black Eyed Peas and "Pump It."

BROWN COW

INGREDIENTS

1 ounce coffee liqueur

4 ounces milk

INSTRUCTIONS
Serve over ice in a trough.

HOW BADLY YOU NEED THIS DRINK

THE BUSINESS TRIP

As if she doesn't feel guilty enough when she leaves you for work every day, now Mommy's got to take care of business in a different time zone. After an embarrassing incident at security involving her breast pump ("Well, sir, this actually *prevents* explosions"), she makes it to her destination, where she compulsively checks her phone in case of an emergency, spending her entire 401(k) in roaming charges. A day of meetings is followed by a night of client schmoozery, but all she wants to do is jump on Skype and judge what outfit Daddy's put you in (please, God, not that "pimp-in-training" Adidas tracksuit again). When she finally gets back to her room to deflate the Dolly Partons her colleagues have been ogling, it pains her to flush that liquid gold down the drain because anything more than three ounces of breast milk is on the no-fly list. At the airport, Mommy hits up the duty-free shop to get Daddy a bottle of scotch, which he'll need after his foray into single parenthood. Following some light turbulence during which she was convinced she was going to die in a fiery crash so she hastily wrote out a will on the back of her boarding pass, Mommy arrives home to find you sound asleep and not missing any limbs. It takes every fiber in Mommy's being not to wake you. It's the one time she hopes you won't sleep through the night.

THE IN-FLIGHT COCKTAIL

INGREDIENTS

1 ounce vodka

Champagne

Dash of simple syrup

1 ounce crème de cassis

3 fresh raspberries

Squeeze of lemon

INSTRUCTIONS

Pour the vodka, Champagne, and simple syrup into a glass. Top with the crème de cassis, raspberries, and lemon. Garnish with a swizzle stick, cocktail napkin, and a child kicking your seat.

HOW BADLY YOU NEED THIS DRINK

WARDROBE

Mommy was never living at the height of fashion, but since your birth she's definitely reached new lows. Her closet is a jail cell for fashion crimes, containing hardened criminals like Ann Taylor and Laura Ashley. She wishes she could do a major purge and splurge, but she feels guilty even eyeing those Tory Burch flats in the window of Nordstrom because she should be BOGO-ing at Payless and fixing the leaky basement. Not only does she have zero time to buy new clothes, but when she puts on anything clean you proceed to accessorize it with milky drool, goobery hands, or pee. And honestly? Mommy isn't super psyched about shopping at Lane Bryant, but until she loses this baby weight she doesn't have a lot of options. On weekends, she can get away with wearing the same Banana Republic Factory Store maxidress over and over again, but during the week her coworkers are subjected to a fashion-show Groundhog Day as she rotates five business-passable outfits like days-of-the-week underwear. Speaking of underwear, poor Daddy. Her lingerie drawer is full of threadbare Victoria's Secret, except for the one red thong from last Valentine's Day that still has the tags on it. Daddy can dream.

THE SUPERMODEL'S NIGHTMARE

INGREDIENTS

1 ounce Irish cream

1 ounce crème de cacao

INSTRUCTIONS

Pour over a scoop (or a whole pint) of vanilla
ice cream.

HOW BADLY YOU NEED THIS DRINK

DISPOSABLE INCOME

Before you were born, Mommy and Daddy were living like assholes. Two thriving careers and no kids meant lavish dinners out, resorts with swim-up bars, and ironic hats. The financial meltdown began with all the crud Mommy had to buy for you that you really didn't need, like the forty-seven newborn Onesies you outgrew on day two and every Fisher-Price contraption ever invented. Maternity leave's nosedive into the red was only outdone by the euro debt crisis. She's suddenly found herself more broke than when she worked as an intern and lived off canned corn but without the benefit of creepy old men paying for her drinks. Even though she's now back to work, the cost of child care alone means she's barely able to claw her way back to solvency. If only some distant relative would materialize out of nowhere to bail her out with a multimillion-dollar inheritance, she could finally fix the GODDAMNED LEAKY BASEMENT. Or at least buy a decent pair of non-elastic-waist pants.

THE LAYAWAY

INGREDIENTS

1 ounce melon liqueur

1 ounce lemon vodka

3 ounces cranberry juice

Splash of coconut water

INSTRUCTIONS

Fill a disposable cup (if you can afford one) with ice.
Pour in all the ingredients and stir.

HOW BADLY YOU NEED THIS DRINK

 BRUNCH

For the attractive, single crowd, Sunday brunch is held around 1 PM. However, family-friendly brunch, where the restaurant is overrun with screaming children and nary an awkward one-night stand is in sight, is at 9 AM. Mommy is starving by then, having been up since the crack of stupid, but at least at that hour there are fewer hipsters giving her the stink eye. Actually, the only person there with a hangover is the waiter/drama major who looks like he wants to off himself. Mommy can smell last night's rye and ginger seeping out of his pores. (And for a split second she is actually tempted to lick his arm just to get a taste of last night's shenanigans. God, she needs to get out more.) At first you are well-behaved as Failed Actor performs his obligatory, "Oh how cute, do you want a mimosa little man? Ha ha ha" routine, but before Mommy even gets a hit of caffeine you're flinging rice cakes, or you're smashing the bread plate, or you've taken an epic shit. Mommy is determined to finish her Eggs Florentine, and it's Romper Room hour right now anyway, so she apologizes profusely and endures the "you-are-tipping-me-30-percent" death glare. And she does, even though she's 100 percent sure he spit in her home fries.

THE COOL CROWD CAPPUCCINO

(If you can't sit next to them anymore, you might as well enjoy their drink of choice.)

INGREDIENTS

1 ounce vodka

½ ounce crème de cacao

1 ounce hot espresso

Frothy, warm milk

Freshly grated nutmeg

INSTRUCTIONS

In a mug, combine the vodka, crème de cacao, and hot espresso with the milk. Dust with nutmeg and irony.

HOW BADLY YOU NEED THIS DRINK

HOLIDAYS

As if the role of parent wasn't already a full-time gig, for the first time in her life Mommy is now also expected to wear the hats of Easter Bunny, Halloween Witch, and Santa Claus. Given these milestones will most likely be erased from your young memory before Mommy's paid the resulting Visa bill, the endgame of these momentous first holidays is to capture the perfect photo. Unfortunately for all mankind, they involve you perched in a pumpkin patch or adorned in a pastel Onesie with bunny tail. Said photos come at a hefty price, usually paid in Mommy sweat and tears. Take your Baby's First Christmas photo. Even though she knows better, Mommy waited until the very last minute to get this done, which meant circling the mall parking lot for twenty minutes and waiting in line for more than an hour as your mail-order elf outfit became increasingly soaked with drool. Mommy knows you're currently suffering from a raging case of separation anxiety, but handed you to a portly stranger with a foot-long white beard anyway and was shocked when you burst into hysterical tears. Mommy was (surprise!) upgraded to the Gold package at the cash register, because ten crying photos of you and a keepsake ornament are better than one. After enduring other preholiday pain, including the in-laws and a smackdown at Toys "R" Us, Mommy wishes she could book a spontaneous Christmas Eve flight to Jamaica. Instead, the week will be spent schlepping you from one obligatory family event to the next. The holidays used to be about watching crazy Uncle Carl get drunk, work parties, and taking advantage of the sales. Now it's about not scarring your childhood, dodging unsolicited parenting advice from the relatives, and deep breathing.

* BUZZKILL ALERT: Our lawyers "suggest" caution in consuming raw eggs due to the slight risk of salmonella.

"DON'T FERTILIZE MY EGG!" NOG

(If you're not pregnant this holiday season,
bust out the raw eggs* and alcohol.)

INGREDIENTS

8 eggs, separated

⅓ cup plus 1 tablespoon sugar

4 cups whole milk

1 cup heavy cream

1 cup bourbon

1 tablespoon vanilla extract

Loads of freshly grated nutmeg

INSTRUCTIONS

In the bowl of a stand mixer, beat the egg yolks until they lighten in color. Gradually add ⅓ cup sugar and continue to beat until it is completely dissolved. Add the milk, cream, bourbon, vanilla, and nutmeg and stir to combine.

Place the egg whites in a separate bowl of a stand mixer and beat to soft peaks. With the mixer running, gradually add the remaining 1 tablespoon of sugar and beat until stiff peaks form. Fold the egg whites into the egg yolk mixture. Chill and serve.

NOTE

Serves 8. Don't serve to Uncle Carl.

HOW BADLY YOU NEED THIS DRINK

THE NANNY

Mommy has an unhealthy crush on the Nanny. She can see why Jude Law went astray. This magical woman not only takes care of you all day, but she also manages to tidy the house, do the laundry, and prepare meals—a feat Mommy told Daddy was "not humanly possible, so stop asking." A total stranger when Mommy first placed you in her arms, she is now one of Mommy's top three people in the world, often hedging out Daddy for second place. However, the Nanny is also the reason you will be going to Online U instead of the London School of Economics. She costs an absolute fortune. Mommy is jealous that the Nanny is teaching you how to say your first words and gets to take you on playdates (aka snoop on neighbors' houses). Mommy wishes she could spend all day with you, but instead she has to sit in back-to-back meetings about optimizing meetings. Even though Mommy is eternally grateful for this woman who gives you such wonderful care, if you so much as hint that you love her more, Mommy's got the INS on speed dial.

THE BLOODY MARY POPPINS

INGREDIENTS

Lemon juice

Celery salt

1 ounce vodka

3 ounces tomato juice

Dash of Worcestershire sauce

Pinch of salt and freshly ground pepper

Tabasco sauce

1 celery stalk

INSTRUCTIONS

Rim a glass with lemon juice, then celery salt, and
fill it with ice. Pour in the vodka and the tomato
and lemon juices. Add the Worcestershire, salt and
pepper, and Tabasco to taste. Garnish with the celery
stalk. Chase with a spoonful of sugar.

HOW BADLY YOU NEED THIS DRINK

DADDY

From the outside, having a baby didn't really change Daddy's life all that much. Physically, he didn't have his penis ripped in half delivering you, though he did put on a few pounds in "sympathy weight," aka "excuse to eat more chicken wings." Daddy can still drink when it pleases him, not having to worry about incubating a human being or feeding you from his man boobs. He didn't have to put his career on hold to take what he once jokingly referred to as "staycation." (Daddy learned the hard way never to make that *hilarious* joke again.) No one asks him if he suffers from debilitating guilt when leaving you to go to work, and in fact, becoming a father only upped his cred as a corporate man. To be fair, it's not all rainbows and unicorns for Daddy—he too has to get up at Early as Fuck O'Clock and his man cave is now your nursery. Gone are the days of drinking Champagne off Mommy's naked body on a Tuesday. Now he has to put up with Mommy flying off the handle because he put the forks away incorrectly. She's lucky he hasn't "gone for smokes," never to be seen again. Mommy may not say it often enough, but she loves Daddy a whole lot.

A MAN-HATTAN

INGREDIENTS

1½ ounces rye

½ ounce sweet vermouth

2 dashes of bitters

Cherry

INSTRUCTIONS

Combine all the ingredients in a shaker with ice.
Shake well, strain, and pour into a glass. Garnish
with a cherry. Serve it to Daddy. He's earned it.

HOW BADLY YOU NEED THIS DRINK

"WHEN ARE YOU HAVING A SECOND?"

Mommy had barely issued your birth announcement when people started asking her when she was going to give you a little brother or sister. Now that your first birthday is approaching, Mommy can't go a day without being confronted with the question. It comes from all directions—in-laws, colleagues, a middle-aged guy in the Starbucks line—and it's almost always accompanied by unsolicited advice about the importance of perfectly timing the age difference between siblings (according to the latest perspective on the subject from a totally credible news source like Tori Spelling's Twitter feed). But the question most often comes from other new Mommies, disguised as actual interest in Mommy's life but truly a cry for help along the lines of: "If I'm going down this miserable road again, this time with toddler in tow, you better the hell be coming along with me!" Even worse than the questions are the prying eyes, scanning Mommy's midsection for clues and monitoring her wine consumption at social events, forcing her to make a big production of pouring herself a second glass of Cabernet, which then haunts her the next morning when you wake up at 5 AM. Though several women from her prenatal class are already aglow with swollen ankles and pregnancy acne again, Mommy is simply not ready. Yet.

ONE-HIT WONDER

INGREDIENTS

1 ounce Irish cream

INSTRUCTIONS

Fill a short glass with ice. Pour in the Irish cream
and consume while listening to the sweet sounds of
Deee-Lite, Take That, or Vanilla Ice.

NOTE

Whoever said "the more, the merrier" never
endured nine months of pregnancy.

HOW BADLY YOU NEED THIS DRINK

SINGLE PEOPLE

If you can sleep in, spend $26 on lemon sage ravioli, fly last minute to Croatia, get your eyebrows waxed, have nothing in your fridge but Stella Artois and mustard, take Yoga Muay Thai Fusion Wednesdays at 6 PM, say things like "This season of *Walking Dead* was staid and uninspired and couldn't live up to neoclassical themes woven into the existential tapestry of *Game of Thrones*," or own nice things, then you are single. Single people complain about being single all the time. Mommy nods politely as they whine about eHarmony, their cat's digestive issues, or the end of a Tribeca Film Festival selection, but all the while Mommy is fantasizing about wearing their skin to become them, just like in *The Silence of the Lambs*. Single people don't pee when they sneeze. They really don't know how good they have it. This, of course, does not apply to single parents, who are heroes and should be given keys to the city's wine cellar immediately.

THE CØSMØMPØLITAN

1 ounce mandarin vodka

½ ounce cherry vodka

½ ounce Cointreau

Splash of lime juice

Splash of pomegranate juice

INSTRUCTIONS

Combine all the ingredients in a shaker with ice.
Shake well and strain into a glass.

NOTE

The traditional Cosmo may be the single girl's
go-to drink, but this delicious tipple is just
for you.

HOW BADLY YOU NEED THIS DRINK

BATH TIME

Nothing used to make Mommy feel more relaxed than a bath. Bubbles, lavender-scented candles, and some Sade were all she needed to unwind. Now bath time gives Mommy several mini–heart attacks (fear of hypothermia/drowning/soap blindness), and it's worse now that you keep trying to stand (fear of splitting head open on Moen faucet). Mommy is not sure who is more soaking after tub time, you or her. Then the other day you "dropped some kids off at the pool." Weird face + making your own bubbles = suddenly you're bathing in feces. Mommy briefly felt triumphant after she successfully held you squirming and slippery while using the massage feature on the hand wand to beat last night's mushy peas down the drain. Then you peed on her.

LIQUID DRANO

INGREDIENTS

1 ounce light rum

1 ounce blueberry schnapps

3 ounces blue Gatorade

Frozen blueberries

INSTRUCTIONS

Fill a highball glass with ice. Pour in the rum,
schnapps, and Gatorade and stir. Garnish with
blueberries. Enjoy on a nonslip surface.

HOW BADLY YOU NEED THIS DRINK

MEAL PLANNING

Mommy didn't know how good she had it during your first few months of life, when the only thought she had to put into meal planning was whether to offer you the right or the left breast first (and even that she got wrong half the time). Your voyage into the world of solids started with the puree phase, where Mommy learned that her blender had functionality beyond margarita making. Unfortunately, just when she had finally perfected her sweet potato–banana–pea medley, it was time to move on to more substantial solids. This meant brushing up on the baby Heimlich, bracing for new surprises in your diaper, and learning whether this self-directed feeding craze would be as horribly messy as it sounded. (Check.) Mommy's fantasies of preparing a week's worth of elaborate meals every Sunday afternoon died before she finished typing "Baby + Meals" into Google. In real life, meal preparation involves cutting up whatever random assortment of fruits and vegetables happen to be in the crisper into bite-sized pieces, at least 50 percent of which end up on the floor. The books say this will get easier in a few months when you'll be able to eat everything Mommy does. Sadly, Mommy's pretty sure that a diet of frozen pizzas and Häagen-Dazs bars do not the next Bill Gates make, and she's counting on you to make her dreams of early retirement come true.

PARENTIÑA COLADA

INGREDIENTS

1 ounce light rum

3 tablespoons coconut cream

3 tablespoons crushed pineapple

2 cups ice

INSTRUCTIONS

Bust out the blender and dump all the ingredients inside. Let the sound of the whirring motor bring you back to all-inclusive trips of days gone by when the only planning you had to do was deciding which minidress to wear to the foam party.

HOW BADLY YOU NEED THIS DRINK

YOU'RE A HAIR PULLER

Mommy was already a fringe member of the neighborhood Mommy circles, given her lackluster baking skills and shameful habit of dressing you in sleepers at all hours of the day, well beyond the three-month grace period. But now you've sealed her social fate as a Mommy pariah with your newfound hair-pulling fixation. Unfortunately, Mommy's desperate cries of "Gentle! Gentle!" only make you pull your victim in closer, until Mommy is forced to pry you away, beg for forgiveness, and then disappear with you into the night, her head bowed in shame. Mommy thought hairless babies were safe from your iron fist, but apparently you don't distinguish between a handful of hair and scalp. Even more upsetting than the trauma you've inflicted on your former playmates is Mommy's realization that, for the rest of her life, any bad behavior you engage in will always reflect on her and something she should or shouldn't have done/said/taught/discouraged/encouraged/practiced. Mommy wants to pull her hair out just thinking about it.

THE LONELY ISLAND

(nonalcoholic)

INGREDIENTS

2 ounces coconut milk

2 ounces lime juice

Sparkling water

Sprig of fresh mint

INSTRUCTIONS

Combat baby-induced social isolation by getting
in touch with your inner Tom Hanks with this
Castaway-inspired mocktail. Chill a tall glass and
fill it with ice. Combine the coconut milk and lime
juice in a shaker, and pour into the glass. Fill with
sparkling water, stir, and garnish with the mint. If
you're feeling lonely these days, befriend a volleyball.
"Wilsonnnnnnnnn!"

HOW BADLY YOU NEED THIS DRINK

PHOTOGRAPHY

One of the unwritten commandments of parenthood is "Thou shalt digitally capture every waking moment of your child's first year of life." This means Mommy and Daddy are perpetually lugging around the ten-pound Canon EOS-can't-believe-how-much-they-paid-for-this-when-they-only-use-the-auto-function-Rebel T4i everywhere you go. They have also been forced to purchase multiple external hard drives to store the 198,736 high-res photos of you that Mommy plans to organize sometime between now and her retirement, not to mention all the photos from Mommy's previous life featuring her, a throng of girls clad in minidresses, and a bottle of Prosecco. Although she maxed out her Visa printing the best (read: every) photo of you in month one, at least she didn't succumb to one of those newborn photo shoots, with their overuse of props and poses that involve curling you naked into flowerpots like a demented Anne Geddes tribute. Seeing those kinds of photos in her Facebook newsfeed before bedtime is a guaranteed recipe for nightmares and ruthless unfriending action. Mommy has opted to keep you off Facebook altogether to protect your privacy.* Anyway, Mommy can't keep up with the extensive Instagramming now required before a photo is deemed Facebook ready. Why does every baby now look like it was born in 1977? At least now that photo postproduction is socially acceptable, Mommy can delete the massive bags from under her eyes before applying the Sutro effect.

---

* Actual reason: to pretend she's still single and twenty-three.

INSTA-GRAHAM SHOT

INGREDIENTS

Chocolate syrup

Graham cracker crumbs

1 ounce marshmallow vodka

½ ounce chocolate liqueur

½ ounce Irish cream

INSTRUCTIONS

Rim a shot glass with chocolate syrup and then
graham cracker crumbs. Combine the vodka,
chocolate liqueur, and Irish cream in a shaker with
ice. Shake well and strain into the shot glass.

NOTE

Now that's a perfect shot.

HOW BADLY YOU NEED THIS DRINK

୧୧ THE PEDIATRICIAN ୧୧

Mommy's lucky if she makes it to her annual physical every three years. But now every other month she's trucking you to the pediatrician, forcing her to confront some of her greatest maternal fears head on: fear of side effects from your vaccinations. Fear of the splinter-rific rocking horse in the waiting area. Even the twenty-five-year-old receptionist with the perma-frown frightens the hell out of her. Mommy honestly can't think of a more physically and emotionally taxing way to spend a Friday morning. And she's not even the one getting a needle shoved into her thigh. After an excruciating hour wait (spent desperately trying to keep you from manhandling the toddler with the hacking cough), Mommy's too drained to remember all the burning questions she prepared. Like should she have called poison control when you drank some of your No More Tears baby shampoo last week, and will you still become a Rhodes Scholar if the only thing she can get you to eat for dinner lately is cheese? At least Mommy can satisfy her inner nerd with your height and weight percentile scores. Finally some payoff for those 3 AM feedings!

THE DOCTOR'S ORDER

INGREDIENTS

1 ounce vodka

4 ounces orange juice

2 ounces Dr Pepper

INSTRUCTIONS

Fill a glass with ice. Pour in all the ingredients and
stir. Enjoy with an apple and WebMD.

HOW BADLY YOU NEED THIS DRINK

69

BABY PROOFING

Mommy's not sure how her pretty little house turned into Alcatraz overnight. Everywhere she turns, Mommy is intercepted by bars, latches, or clamps. Even the toilet seat is equipped with an industrial-grade lock. Mommy can't get into anything these days without breaking a nail, spraining an ankle, or seeking help from an instructional video on YouTube. And the price for her *CSI: Sesame Street* home makeover? Seven hundred dollars and an entire weekend devoted to installation. Mommy thought nothing could be more excruciating than the hours she spent sifting through hundreds of Benjamin Moore paint chips and every issue of *Elle Decor* to land on the perfect off-white hue for every wall and piece of trim. Until she had to watch Daddy drill unsightly holes into half of the fruits of her labor to install baby gates that you'll conquer in approximately three days. Not so long ago, Mommy would have thought that any parent who would go to such extreme precautionary measures to protect his or her child must be suffering from a severe paranoia disorder. Then she turned her back on you for five seconds last week and caught you halfway up the staircase about to empty the contents of her change purse into your mouth. Safety first: 1, Mommy: 0.

ALABAMA SLAMMER

INGREDIENTS

1 ounce Southern Comfort

1 ounce Amaretto

Dash of grenadine

4 ounces orange juice

INSTRUCTIONS

Fill a glass with ice. Pour in the Southern Comfort, Amaretto, and grenadine. Top off with the orange juice and stir. Dream about life on the outside.

HOW BADLY YOU NEED THIS DRINK

70

⎰ YOUR FIRST BIRTHDAY ⎱

As adult birthday celebrations fade into oblivion only to emerge once a decade tainted with flamingos, over-the-hill cards, and awkward-for-everyone mooning incidents, birthday parties have come to entail sacrificing your afternoon nap every other Saturday to witness the ultimate battle for gold in the Mommylympic games. As your first birthday approaches, Mommy begins to panic. Surfing inspiration boards on Pinterest is the anti-help with its tiered princess cake recipes, twenty-three-step guides to hand-making party favors, and links to customized invitation websites with four-week delivery lead times. Banking on the limitations of your one-year-old memory, Mommy resorts to her only options at the eleventh hour: Evite's first birthday party template, Dollar Store decor, and a supermarket cake. A year ago today, Mommy was in labor, but right now the only thing she's giving birth to is a massive migraine. As a pack of wild wolves* descends on her house on party day, Mommy silently bids farewell to her pearl white couch cover while cursing the Italian who decided that pizza sauce should be red. After the festivities conclude with present opening, during which Mommy attempts to exude excitement upon opening yet another regifted copy of *Goodnight Moon,* you are exhausted, and for the first time in months you fall asleep in Mommy's arms. Staring at you at that moment, it hits Mommy that her little baby is no longer a baby. Although her type A personality would normally propel her to hand you to Daddy and immediately launch into cleaning her tornado-ravaged living room, Mommy nestles into the icing-encrusted couch cushions and savors this moment a little while longer.

* Fifteen children under the age of five and their parents.

THE CONFETTI COCKTAIL

(nonalcoholic)

INGREDIENTS

4 ounces unsweetened cherry cider

1 ounce almond syrup

1 apple, peeled, cored, and cubed

1 pear, peeled, cored, and cubed

1 peach, peeled, pitted, and cubed

INSTRUCTIONS

Combine all the ingredients in a blender with ice and blend until smooth. Pour into a glass and consume while doing internal cartwheels because you're not in labor today.

HOW BADLY YOU NEED THIS DRINK

71

WEANING

In the latest installment of the dramatic series known as *Mommy Is Essentially a Talking Barn Animal,* the time has come to wean you. Weaning is the universe's way of telling Mommy that the party is officially over: "Time to hand over that free boob job you've been enjoying. Oh, and don't forget to pick up your period on your way out." If busting out her 32B bra collection wasn't punishment enough, Mommy also has to deal with Daddy gloating about the fact that she can no longer say things like: "Can you make me an elaborate four-course meal? I would do it, but I have to nurse the baby." However, at least she can go back to the old standby: "Can you make me an elaborate four-course meal? I would do it, but I have girl-time cramps." Thank God men don't understand Women's Troubles. As much as she's looking forward to burning her Bravado bras, Mommy already misses nursing. It was that special thing that only she could share with you. She hereby promises to never be judgy about mothers who breast-feed their school-aged children again. Keep the party goin' and the liquid a-flowin', sisters!

THE MAD COW

INGREDIENTS

Chocolate syrup

½ ounce coffee liqueur

½ ounce hazelnut liqueur

½ ounce vodka

½ ounce Irish cream

3 ounces milk

Whipped cream

INSTRUCTIONS

Drizzle chocolate syrup around the rim of a glass.
Combine the coffee and hazelnut liqueurs, vodka,
Irish cream, and milk in a shaker with ice. Shake
well and strain into the glass. Top the mixture with
whipped cream. Now scrape off all that whipped
cream because you're no longer burning five hundred
calories a day. "Moo!" (said angrily).

HOW BADLY YOU NEED THIS DRINK

72

✑ YOUR FIRST HAIRCUT ✑

It's clear the time has come for your ceremonial first haircut. Mommy's been avoiding this day, but it's not because she's using you as a pawn in an elaborate gender experiment. (Not that there's anything wrong with that.) (No, actually, there is.) It's just that, thanks to the booming baby industry, any milestone in your life always makes Mommy feel like she's got "I'm a new parent: Overcharge me" tattooed across her forehead. Mommy considered taking matters into her own hands until Daddy pointed out that anyone who outsources her own eyebrow maintenance shouldn't be trusted with a pair of scissors and an infant's head. So now Mommy finds herself at what is known in yuppie Mommyland as a Children's Hair Salon. It's great to see that, despite the hefty price premium versus Magicuts, the family-friendly salon is equipped without changing tables (!). After changing you on her thigh and ruining a perfectly not good pair of jeans, Mommy asks the stylist where to dispose of your diaper. Mommy is given a look like she's just asked Bret Michaels if she could shove the hot mess under his bandanna. Only less into it. At least Mommy leaves with a photo of you (crying) and a First Haircut Certificate (hot tip: they're available free online), both of which will get prime placement in the "Look! I'm a great parent!" album that you'll be forced to review on your thirteenth birthday. At which time, in a cruel twist of fate, Mommy will probably be begging you to cut your hair.

THE IRONIC COCKTAIL

INGREDIENTS

1 ounce pomegranate liqueur

2 ounces orange juice

3 ounces sparkling wine

Zest of orange

INSTRUCTIONS

Pour the pomegranate liqueur, orange juice, and
sparkling wine into a Champagne flute. Garnish with
the orange zest and toast to Alanis Morissette and
the famous chopping of her waist-long locks.

HOW BADLY YOU NEED THIS DRINK

73

SIPPY CUPS

Mommy always thought the biggest challenge she would face as a parent would be a momentous one, like guiding your moral compass or steering you away from a career in the arts. Instead, her most significant parenting feat has been finding you a sippy cup that actually functions properly. Every one of the fifteen models Mommy has purchased yields the same result: you wearing a soaking wet "My Dad Is Rad" T-shirt, finger painting in a $6 puddle of organic milk. The fact that none of them works makes their complicated design all the more mind-boggling. Mommy could have taught you quantum physics with the energy she's expended digging through drawers in search of an elusive straw, lid, or flow valve. Meanwhile, the only cup you're ever interested in is either a fragile heirloom filled with scalding coffee or one pried from the snotty hand of the kid at the park with the raging cold. Mommy needs her own sippy cup, stat.

THE GROWN-UP GOBLET

INGREDIENTS

1 ounce dark rum

½ ounce coconut liqueur

½ ounce coffee liqueur

1 ounce lemon juice

4 ounces pineapple juice

INSTRUCTIONS

Combine the rum, coconut and coffee liqueurs, and
the lemon and pineapple juices in a shaker with ice.
Shake well and serve in nature's sippy cup: a coconut.

HOW BADLY YOU NEED THIS DRINK

 GADGETS

If your recent obsession with electronics is giving you a head start on a lucrative career in electrical engineering, Mommy is 100 percent supportive. And she definitely appreciates that you helped her discover 90 percent of her iPhone's functionality. She just wishes you could at least pretend to be interested in the mountain of expensive Playskool lying untouched on the living room floor. Unfortunately, your ideal toy these days meets at least two of the following criteria:

1. Has lots of buttons for you to press incessantly
2. If broken, will cost lots of money to repair or will threaten Mommy's job security
3. Ceases to function when dropped in the toilet

Mommy thought she was doing the right thing by trolling the aisles of Target for a plastic phone that would distract you from hers. But, according to *Wired,* she should have spent that time embracing your iPhone fixation by downloading the top-rated app for babies. How else are you going to learn to speak Mandarin, get up to speed on the socioeconomic undercurrent in Sierra Leone, and figure out how to unlock the Angry Birds "Chrome Dimension" levels by the age of two? Truthfully, Mommy finds it a bit disconcerting that you're already more tech savvy than she and that you and your cohort will render her generation obsolete by 2029.

CREAMY CARAMEL APPLETINI

INGREDIENTS

1 ounce caramel Irish cream

½ ounce apple vodka

½ ounce apple schnapps

Slice of apple

Caramel sauce

INSTRUCTIONS

Combine the Irish cream, vodka, and schnapps in a shaker with ice. Shake well and strain into a martini glass. Garnish with an apple slice and drizzle with the caramel sauce. When life hands you a toilet-water-damaged Apple™, make a martini.

HOW BADLY YOU NEED THIS DRINK

TEETHING

Teething is the Get Out of Jail Free card bestowed to babies. Up at midnight, 2 AM, and 5 AM for a week straight, after you'd finally learned to sleep through the night? *It must be teething.* Bit Sofia's finger at swim class? *It must be teething.* Bad case of baby PMS? *It must be teething.* If you actually sprouted a tooth every time Mommy uttered those four words, you could buy the family the 2020 Dodge Grand Caravan with the jackpot you've got coming from the tooth fairy. Mommy only wishes the misery ended when those pearly whites poked through your little gums. Unfortunately, even though they are merely stand-ins, those baby teeth need brushing—a process that goes down something like this: Mommy comes at you with the Elmo toothbrush. You and Mommy play tug-of-war with the toothbrush. Mommy wins because she's bigger. Mommy attempts to pry your lips open long enough to run the brush at least once along your top and bottom gums. You let out a bloodcurdling scream. Mommy loses because she has a headache. You lick the organic fluoride-free berry-flavored tooth gel off the brush and fling it under the toilet. Mommy gives up and adds baby gingivitis to the ever-growing list of things that keep her up at night.

THE PEARLY GATE

INGREDIENTS

1 ounce vodka

1 ounce white crème de cacao

3 ounces milk

INSTRUCTIONS

Combine all the ingredients in a shaker with ice.
Shake well and strain into a large glass.

NOTE

Your drink can be the perfect shade of white,
even if your baby's teeth can't.

HOW BADLY YOU NEED THIS DRINK

‿‿ BOARD BOOKS ‿‿

At least the name is accurate. After reading *Big Red Barn* for the 1,098th time, Mommy is officially bored. She used to pore over Jonathan Franzen novels and biographies about Steve Jobs, but now she finds herself overly invested in the search-and-rescue mission unfolding in *Where's Spot?* This is not helping her reverse the rapid descent into permanent Mommy Brain. Some board books don't even have plots. Or words! They're just pictures of babies next to pictures of baby animals. How did this author get a book deal? Did she go into Random House and say, "I'll shoot you straight. I spent my advance on a cocaine-fueled gambling binge, but check out these royalty-free stock shots I found on Google Images"? To spice things up, Mommy has started going off script and hoping you don't notice. In last night's rendition of *Goodnight Moon,* the Quiet Old Lady was having a torrid affair with the Cow, and the two Little Kittens were about to expose the scandal on E! Bowl Full of Mush Network. Speaking of *Goodnight Moon,* the page that says "goodnight nobody"? That's messed up. Truthfully, Mommy knows that time passes all too quickly and soon you'll grow out of her reading to you. Then she'll miss Sandra Boynton's complexities of the postmodern antihero in *The Snuggle Puppy.* One day you'll read *Charlotte's Web* all on your own. SPOILER ALERT: The central character *dies.* This is why you should stick to math.

BOARD BOOK EMPIRE

INGREDIENTS

1 ounce Canadian Club whisky

1 ounce peach schnapps

3 ounces cola

Squeeze of lime

INSTRUCTIONS

Fill a glass with ice. Pour in all the ingredients
and stir. Serve on a board book, which makes a
great coaster.

HOW BADLY YOU NEED THIS DRINK

GROCERY SHOPPING

Grocery shopping used to mean languidly browsing the aisles of Whole Paycheck, buying organic hempseed granola, sampling cold-pressed virgin olive oils, and sipping on a freshly juiced beetroot frappé. However, since you were born, Mommy's had to switch to the discount supermarket chain, and bringing you there with her is an epic test of patience. Uh-oh. Your diaper drawer is running on empty and the only thing in the fridge is a flaccid zucchini so she's forced to load you in the car and take a deep breath. Gone are the days of carefully reviewing ingredient lists and doing price-per-ounce comparisons on the six offerings of salsa in the Mexican food aisle. It's a race against the clock à la Supermarket Sweep to load the shopping cart before you have a meltdown and/or hurl a carton of eggs all over aisle four. Mommy is appalled that she's about to buy a $19 dress that's displayed next to a pyramid of Charmin, but the five outfits she's had on rotation since returning to work are literally disintegrating. Hey cool! The section of her wallet that used to be reserved for receipts for pretty, breakable things is now loaded up with coupons for diaper wipes and grocery points cards. In a true testament to her devotion to your nap schedule, Mommy flings her (much-needed) Lady Speed Stick to the wayside so she can use the express checkout. Because if you fall asleep in the car seat before she makes it home, she'll be forced to drive up and down the highway for two hours while the Cherry Garcia melts all over the trunk.

AMAZON LEMONADE

INGREDIENTS

1 ounce vodka

4 ounces pink lemonade

Wedge of lemon

INSTRUCTIONS

Fill a tall glass with ice, add the vodka, top off with lemonade, and garnish with a lemon wedge. It's time to embrace online shopping.

HOW BADLY YOU NEED THIS DRINK

WORKING FROM HOME

Sometimes the basement floods or the nanny gets deported and suddenly Mommy is forced to work from home. This usually coincides with the worst possible day ever to be out of the office. You're happily playing on the floor, so she orchestrates a conference call.

MOMMY: Thanks, everyone, for dialing in. As you can see on slide four—

YOU: DUCKA DUCKA DUCKAAAAAAAAAA!

CLIENT: Is there a fire alarm on your end?

ACCOUNT GUY: I think I hear a cat dying.

Mommy quickly turns on Sesame Street's YouTube channel, even though it might give you epilepsy, and goes off the cuff because she can't see her PowerPoint.

MOMMY: As you'll see on slide six—

CLIENT: What happened to slide four?

You spill organic goat milk all over Mommy's laptop. Sad Mac face appears.

MACBOOK AIR: BLEEEEEERRRRRRR!

YOU: BLEEEEEERRRRRRR!

ACCOUNT GUY: Seriously, is that cat okay?

Mommy tries to hit Mute but instead hangs up. Now she can't find the passcode because you ate the piece of paper it was written on. When she finally dials back in, she has no idea what anyone is talking about. It's probably about her.

CLIENT: . . . clear out the dead weight, we'll be in a great place. What do you think on your end?

MOMMY: Well . . . (*fuuuuck!*) . . . let's circle back COB with some below-the-line ideas to maximize share of dollar (*that sounds like Mommy has this under control, right?*).

Total silence.

YOU: PPPFFFTTTTTTTTWRRRAAAAPPPFFFTTTTTTT!

Mercifully, someone has a hard stop so the call ends. Your diaper has leaked all over the sofa. Mommy lies down on it anyway. Later you pick up her company-owned BlackBerry and toss it in the toilet, which is a good metaphor for where Mommy's career is headed.

CAREER SUICIDE

INGREDIENTS

1 ounce Malibu rum

1 ounce tequila

3 ounces lemon-lime soda

Splash of orange juice

Splash of grenadine

INSTRUCTIONS

Combine all ingredients in an ice-filled glass and stir.
Enjoy while surfing Monster.com.

HOW BADLY YOU NEED THIS DRINK

9 PM

Nine o'clock used to be a dinner reservation. Now it's a bedtime. By the time Mommy feeds you squash, washes squash off the wall, and gets you to bed, she has exactly twenty-three minutes to eat whatever you didn't in front of *The X-Factor* before she passes out with her hair encrusted in squash. Being up at 2 AM used to mean it was a good night. Now it's a very, very bad night. It means Mommy will also be up at 3 AM, up at 4 AM, and up for good at 6 AM. Those wee hours used to be for flirting with the bartender to keep the drinks flowing while sexting her backup plan for a booty call. Now she spends that time praying you will go back to sleep while texting her sleep-challenged Mommy friends and cursing the "bulletproof" *No-Cry Sleep Solution* and Daddy's ability to sleep through anything. Sometimes, when Mommy's in line for her fourth Americano Misto of the day, she'll overhear a twenty-something lament being "soooo exhausted." When Mommy was single, "exhaustion" referred to a state of ennui that came from being bored with skinny jeans and dating guys with ironic mustaches. Mommy misses that kind of tired.

THE AFTER EIGHT

INGREDIENTS

1 ounce crème de cacao

1 ounce crème de menthe

Splash of milk

INSTRUCTIONS

Fill a glass with ice. Pour in all the ingredients and stir. Enjoy after 8 PM but before 9 PM lest you turn into a sleep-deprived gremlin the next day.

HOW BADLY YOU NEED THIS DRINK

THE GYM MEMBERSHIP

During a moment of postpartum weakness, Mommy was seduced by a sandwich board outside the local fitness club advertising low membership fees without any initiation charges or commitments. She was also seduced by the club's free "child care" (translation: one exhausted Russian woman and thirty-eight kids running amok in a room smaller, hotter, and germier than the sauna). Later examination of the contract's fine print revealed that Mommy had signed her life away for a free T-shirt, but she was willing to overlook the management's questionable ethics for a chance at scoring the body gracing the promotional flyer. Fast-forward: she's been to the gym exactly twice since your birth and the only thing more painful than walking the next day was the realization that each visit cost her $765. Mommy knows that investing that money in her 401(k) could be her ticket to retiring in Bali. But she's plagued by the fear that throwing in her gym towel could be the gateway to a low-maintenance haircut or buying Crocs. Yes, Mommy is exhausted and time starved, and hasn't picked up an issue of *InStyle* since her first trip to Motherhood Maternity, but if her annual donation to the gym is the price she needs to pay to keep her quest for rock-hard abs alive, Mommy is silencing her inner Suze Orman and holding on to the dream, dammit!

⟋ A SIX-PACK. OF O'DØUL'S. ⟍
(nonalcoholic)

NOTE

0.5% beer. Another way to not get ripped.

HOW BADLY YOU NEED THIS DRINK

FIRST STEPS

If never missing an episode of *Full House* taught Mommy anything, it's that first steps must be captured on film. Back in 1994, this meant recording the moment on a massive camcorder, which Uncle Jesse scored with an original ballad. Today this means archiving the milestone with a slickly edited iMovie cut to Mumford & Sons. As you took your first tentative steps, Mommy's heart swelled with pride. Now it swells with fear. Gone are the days of leaving you in your recalled Bumbo while she "prepared" dinner (read: tossed a frozen pizza in the oven). Walking means you can literally go from 0 to Crashing Through the Screen Door in mere moments. If Hermès made a baby leash she would buy it, but she just can't subject you to the Baby Sherpa Safe2Go Harness fashion blunder. Mommy is already worried that Child Protective Services is going to be called, thanks to the permanent bruise on your forehead from careening into everything. Plus, now that you can walk, your favorite activities include opening every drawer looking for stabby things and going on scavenger hunts for choking hazards. As her eyes fill with tears while you teeter on wobbly knees, Mommy has the distinct feeling that as a teenager, you're going to walk all over her.

WALK 'N' ROLL

INGREDIENTS

1 ounce Johnnie Walker

2 ounces lemonade

2 ounces Red Bull

Wedge of lime

INSTRUCTIONS

Run, don't walk, to the freezer and fill a glass with
ice. Pour in the Johnnie Walker, lemonade, and Red
Bull. Garnish with a lime wedge.

HOW BADLY YOU NEED THIS DRINK

COMPULSIVELY CHECKING
ON YOU WHILE YOU SLEEP

It took forty-five minutes to get you down. It takes forty-five seconds for Mommy to think something has gone wrong.

MOMMY: Do you think the baby's okay?
DADDY: Yes. Do not go back in there. Seriously. Can we please just watch *Duck Dynasty*?

Daddy doesn't understand Mommy Intuition, which he calls Craziness. She says she's just going to listen outside your door, but really she's going on a stealth mission back into your room. Thanks to the baby blackout blinds she can't see if your chest is rising. Nor can she see the Melissa & Doug puzzle piece on the floor, which impales Mommy. She screams internally and, by some miracle, manages not to wake you. Since she's as blind as Snooki's stylist, she tries to listen for your breath. The plush lamb emitting whale sounds (face palm for another toy that will cause you to lag in science) is masking any snores of life. Instead of turning down the orca sheep, she decides it's time to Freak Out and Panic. She frantically grabs you and starts screaming your name. This instantly reveals you're very much alive. Having been woken up from a peaceful slumber by an insane person, you're terrified and bawling your eyes out. Hooray! It's going to be another hour to get you down again, and now she'll never know what the hell *Duck Dynasty* is, but she will repeat this process until you go off to college. At which point she'll continually use all technology available to embarrass you and ensure you're safe.

MOMMY MONITOR SYSTEM

INGREDIENTS

1 ounce vodka

½ ounce triple sec

1 ounce pomegranate juice

Splash of lime juice

Zest of orange

INSTRUCTIONS

Fill a glass with ice. Pour in the vodka, triple sec, and
pomegranate and lime juices and stir. Garnish with
the orange zest.

NOTE

Pairs beautifully with a state-of-the-art baby
monitor, complete with LCD night vision and
false alarms that will cause you to have several
mini–heart attacks.

HOW BADLY YOU NEED THIS DRINK

‿‿ THE PARK ‿‿

When Mommy loads up the stroller with enough crap to open a Babies "R" Us, it means it's time to go to the park. Mommy brought wholesome, organic snacks, but the first thing you do is eat sand. Mmm, notes of raccoon pee. Also, she forgot to pack your hat, which, according to the Unspoken Rules of Parenting, is the equivalent of leaving you outside naked in a snowstorm. At the playground, parenting shortcomings never go unnoticed. Flanked by Stepford Wives who whisper their disapproval and a gaggle of nannies who openly discuss it in a foreign language, Mommy is living an Orwellian existence. At least this means there are lots of other kids for you to play with/catch illnesses from. Including Terror Toddler. Mommy suppresses her inner Jerry Springer and tries not to freak out when this bully-in-training shoves you, snatches your pail, and comes dangerously close to blinding you with a shovel. Who is this kid's parent? Oh, it's Weekend Dad, who is busy texting last night's piece of strange on his hip-holstered Android. Mommy decides to give Terror Toddler a pass, since that kid is going to be filled with self-loathing (and pharmaceuticals) in about a dozen years. Meanwhile, Mommy gets her cardio burn on by chasing you backward up a slide, moving you out of the way of big kids on swings, and catching you from falling off the playground stairs. At least she no longer feels guilty about her lapsed gym membership. Speaking of exercise, now Weekend Dad is doing chin-ups on the monkey bars to impress the local MILFs. Maybe he should spend more time on his parenting skills and less time on his upper-body strength since Terror Toddler is currently aiming a Super Soaker at a sleeping newborn. Oh, the park, where nature and nurture come together to bitch-slap each other in the face.

PARKS AND WRECK

INGREDIENTS

3 ounces lemon juice

2 teaspoons raw sugar

1 ounce light rum

Sprig of fresh basil

INSTRUCTIONS

Rim a glass with some of the lemon juice, then raw
sugar—or with the sand that will permanently be
tracked into your house—and fill the glass with ice.
Pour in the rum, and the rest of the lemon juice and
raw sugar, and stir. Garnish with the basil.

HOW BADLY YOU NEED THIS DRINK

84

ACCELERATED AGING

Like the cast of *Days of Our Lives,* for years Mommy managed to evade the hands of time. Until recently, looking in the bathroom mirror with the dimmer switch fully engaged was like staring at a spitting image of her high-school self (excluding the Sun-In spray damage and fashion crimes involving flannel). But in recent months, the pace at which she's burning through under-eye concealer is giving her hot flashes. Thankfully, Daddy is also aging at the speed of a time-lapse photography sequence in *Planet Earth.* In the most recent round of family portraits, he was a dead ringer for Nick Nolte's infamous mug shot. The next time Mommy impulsively buys a photo package on Groupon, she'll make sure it includes retouching. The sad state of Mommy's skin shouldn't come as much of a surprise, given chronic sleep deprivation and drinking one's weight in coffee once again evaded *Glamour*'s "Top 5 Anti-Aging Secrets" feature this year. And Mommy has spent about as much time tending to her eye area since your birth as she has to understanding the crisis in Syria. Of course you're more than worth every postnatal wrinkle, line, and adult acne scar; Mommy just wishes that on the days when she felt as incompetent as anyone on *Teen Mom,* she at least looked the part.

FOUNTAIN OF YOUTH

(nonalcoholic)

INGREDIENTS

1 cup frozen blueberries

1 cup frozen raspberries

1 ounce pomegranate juice

1 peach, peeled, pitted, and cubed

1 apple, peeled, cored, and cubed

2 cups fresh spinach

2 cups water

INSTRUCTIONS

Combine all the ingredients in a blender and blend until smooth.

NOTE

Loaded with antioxidants, this drink's your best
shot at one day being carded again and still
being able to register excitement on your face
when it happens.

HOW BADLY YOU NEED THIS DRINK

85

THE STROLLER

When you're sixteen and you ask Mommy to help you buy your first set of wheels, Mommy will explain that she already blew way too much cash in that department before you turned sixteen *weeks*. And that doesn't include all the money she's burned on the forty-three accessories purchased to pimp your ride, including cup holders, an arctic foot muff, and a sun hood now covered in Mommy's blood from jamming her finger when she collapsed the stroller for the first time. Nor does it factor in the replacement cost of the countless Robeez shoes, orthodontic pacifiers, and Sophie the Giraffes that you've left littered throughout the neighborhood because your favorite game is launching things overboard and seeing if Mommy notices. (Which she usually doesn't because she's too busy apologizing to other pedestrians for completely monopolizing the sidewalk and/or running over their small dogs.) While Daddy loves talking hydraulics, shocks, and turning radius, Mommy is still haunted by the image of the Bugaboo's price tag. For what they paid that day, Mommy assumed she was wheeling away a magical carriage that would fulfill your every need. Unfortunately, it turns out that a cavalcade of strollers is required: one that's lightweight for navigating the city, one for travel that collapses to the size of an umbrella like a scene out of *The Jetsons,* and even one that Mommy's expected to push while jogging through the city (this one is collecting dust next to her Reebok EasyTone kicks). Then you learned to walk. Now placing you in a stroller of any kind elicits shrieks so bloodcurdling that Mommy regularly checks the seat for sharp objects. Your newfound mobility brings tears to Mommy's eyes—you're all grown up and now it takes forty-five minutes to travel a half block. Wahh!

THE BUGABLUE

INGREDIENTS

1 ounce vodka

1 ounce blue curaçao

3 ounces lemon-lime soda

INSTRUCTIONS

Fill a glass with ice. Pour in all the ingredients and
stir. Serve with a line of credit.

HOW BADLY YOU NEED THIS DRINK

86

SPORTS

Though Mommy was never all that into watching sports, seeing six-packs in high def used to be great motivation to hit the gym the next day. Plus, from the Stanley Cup to the Super Bowl, watching Daddy get all emotionally charged during a playoff game was seriously sexy. But thanks to Mommy's fragile postpartum emotional state, she can barely watch a Cheez Whiz commercial without crying, let alone the next Olympic Games. She's not sure if it's the human interest stories behind these global sporting events that get to her (which always involve some combination of a deceased war hero, a devastating knee injury, and a village fire) or the fact that it's now too late to chase her own athletic dreams (confirmed last week when she pulled a hamstring peeling herself off the couch to microwave a Lean Cuisine). Though at least Mommy feels like she already walked in an Olympian's shoes during her pregnancy, thanks to the dietary restrictions, toting around a shot put for nine months, and a medal-worthy performance in the delivery room. More likely it's because she can't help but wonder if you'll one day grace the cover of *Sports Illustrated* or stand on a podium in front of an audience of billions as she beams with pride from the sidelines. Daddy seems to have also pegged the family's dreams of going pro on you, convinced that an Ivy League scholarship is already in the bag. Mommy secretly wonders if he's reading too much into the "early signs of promise" he's witnessed in you during mealtime, like repeatedly throwing your fusilli at the wall.

GOLD MEDAL COCKTAIL

INGREDIENTS

½ ounce vodka

½ ounce triple sec

3 ounces pureed mango

2 ounces orange juice

Splash of lime

Wedge of lime

INSTRUCTIONS

Combine all the ingredients in an ice-filled glass and
stir. Garnish with a lime wedge.

NOTE

Victory never tasted so sweet.

HOW BADLY YOU NEED THIS DRINK

87

GRANDMA

Your grandma means well, but she's driving Mommy up the (now permanently stained) wall. Apparently, in Grandma's day, children didn't cry, poo, vomit, or do anything other than look like Gerber Baby models. Maybe that's because babies had a pretty good buzz going from the brandy being smeared on their gums. Grandma keeps clearing her throat any time Mommy tries to do anything, which means "You're doing it wrong." Even what Mommy dresses you in is up for scrutiny, like the time she put you in a skull-and-crossbones Onesie from Baby Gap ("Is that a gang shirt? He'll turn to drugs!"). When you were born, she thought Grandma would want to spend time with you so Mommy could nap or shower, or at least pee with the bathroom door closed. But instead Grandma only wanted to hold you when you were sleeping. Mommy still needs Grandma's validation, so she let her feed you meat when you were only three months old ("In my day, babies ate liverwurst sandwiches to build immunity!") and bites her tongue when she gives you inappropriate toys ("It says 'for ages 10 and up,' but how else will the baby learn about sharp edges?"). After never quite outgrowing the scars of her teenage years, Mommy vows to be nothing like Grandma in her parenting choices. However, after catching herself about to chastise you for playing with a color wheel instead of an abacus, she's already started on the rapid descent into her worst nightmare: *becoming her mother.*

THE DUBONNET COCKTAIL

INGREDIENTS

1 ounce Dubonnet Rouge

1 ounce gin

Dash of orange bitters (Or Trop 50)

INSTRUCTIONS

Combine all the ingredients in an ice-filled glass and
stir.

NOTE

These are ingredients most likely found in
Grandma's house, and if you're there, you'll need
a drink immediately.

HOW BADLY YOU NEED THIS DRINK

88

DAY CARE

Alphabet Academy might as well be SoHo House for all the favors Mommy had to call in to snag you a coveted spot in its toddler room. You didn't even have a name (or known gender, as you were the size of an acorn) when Mommy got you spot 256 on the waiting list back when TomKat was still topical. In fact, admission is so competitive that the day care administrator was only the second person (five minutes after Daddy) to find out Mommy was pregnant. Now, more than two years later and just as Mommy was about to take a cue from *Indecent Proposal* to seal the deal once and for all, the day care finally called to confirm your acceptance. Of course, upon hearing the news, other Mommies felt compelled to share unsolicited warnings about the relentless colds and infections that will be inflicted on you, not to mention Mommy and Daddy, for the next year. Mommy refused to believe the haters, until she got the call that you were being sent home with a fever. On day three. Mommy has since had to miss ~~seven~~ two workdays this year (hooray for creative timesheeting!). Mommy truly believes that the structured environment and socialization of day care will benefit you in the long run, but the days when she has to kiss your wet cheeks good-bye at the rainbow-painted door are The Worst.

DAY CARE DEFENSE

INGREDIENTS

1 ounce Cognac

1 ounce light rum

4 ounces orange juice

Zest of orange

INSTRUCTIONS

Fill a glass with ice. Pour in the Cognac, rum, and orange juice and stir. Garnish with orange zest.

NOTE

Numb your guilt, kill germs, and boost your immune system all at once with this triple-duty cocktail.

HOW BADLY YOU NEED THIS DRINK

89

HOUSEGUESTS

Mommy loves seeing her out-of-town friends and relatives. She just wishes it was through the window of the local Hilton. She's still getting used to sharing her tiny space with the entire contents of Babies "R" Us, let alone a family of four and their five-piece Samsonite set. On the day of their arrival, Mommy is forced to spend your coveted nap time Googling family-friendly tourist activities in the area while silently wondering why people on vacation temporarily lose their ability to access the World Wide Web. By day two, the new hardwood floors are covered in scratches from your cousin's counterfeit Thomas the Tank Engine. Mommy should have just gone for Berber. Unfortunately, single houseguests are equally challenging with their oblivion to the choking hazards they leave strewn around the house and their back-to-back social events. Your 6 AM wake-up comes all too soon for Mommy's former college roommate, who noisily made her drunken entrance just an hour earlier following a night on the town to which Mommy was not invited. It's almost as if "I want to spend time with you and your baby" was code for "I want to use your house as a place to store my luggage while I hook up with my ex-boyfriend." Mommy and Daddy are forced to play the Let's Be Quiet game with you in the confines of the basement until she rolls out of bed at noon. At which time she throws up in the kitchen sink, blaming it on the smell of your dirty diapers and not last night's tequila shots. No matter who comes to stay, the house is always depleted of food and cleanliness by the visit's end. As Mommy puts yet another load of sheets into the wash, she actually toys with the idea of having another child sooner than later just so there's no longer a spare bedroom.

THE HOME INVASION

INGREDIENTS

Wedges of lime

Sugar

1 ounce Southern Comfort

1 ounce lime juice

Splash of grenadine

INSTRUCTIONS

Rim a glass with a lime wedge, then sugar, and fill
the glass with ice. Combine the Southern Comfort,
lime juice, and grenadine in a shaker with ice. Shake
well and strain into the glass. Garnish with
a lime wedge.

NOTE

It's the next best thing to the sound of the
airport taxi pulling out of the driveway.

HOW BADLY YOU NEED THIS DRINK

90

MOMMY FEAR

Mommy Fear (MF) is a type of anxiety disorder characterized by crippling paranoia when her baby is not around. MF symptoms manifest when the sufferer is torn from chubby little arms to go to work or a scheduled "I hope Daddy's too tired for sex afterward" date night. Plagued with the fear that no one can offer better child care than she, the MF sufferer conjures up elaborate scenarios that could be playing out in her absence. In an MFer's rational (and in no way neurotic bordering on psychotic) mind, the day care is a covert meth lab, the babysitter is sexting her math teacher, Grandma's gratuitous use of ketchup is causing early-onset diabetes, and Daddy's playing Words with Friends when he's supposed to be watching the baby not eat poison. MF presents in many ways, including compulsively checking one's iPhone and leaving the ringer on high at all times, much to the chagrin of everyone else everywhere. The MF cycle continues well past the toddler stage, peaking during teenage years and lasting forever. Daddy should not attempt to tell the sufferer "Don't worry, the baby's fine," as this could result in his immediate castration. Though MF symptoms can be managed with secret teddy bear cams and hourly FaceTime check-ins, they will never abate. Studies suggest that Mommy will always worry about her child. Always.

THE RX

INSTRUCTIONS

Take a deep breath and enjoy a crisp Chardonnay or
whatever the host is pouring. Enjoy as much of the
glass as you can until MF takes over and you have to
leave the dinner party.

HOW BADLY YOU NEED THIS DRINK

91

‿‿‿‿ THE PLAYDATE ‿‿‿‿

Since your birth, Mommy's formerly enviable social calendar has been reduced to a collection of Playdates. The Playdate forces Mommy to hang out with parents she would usually avoid eye contact with, just because their kids happen to be your age. Occasionally they give Mommy a chance to hang out with parents she likes but whose kids are a few short years away from Ritalin and a stint at Betty Ford. Going on the Playdate does have its perks, such as sizing up other people's kitchen renos and snooping through their bedrooms while "getting lost" en route to the bathroom. At the Playdate, a children's meal is usually served, which is a reflection of the host's parenting choices. Like the "I do whatever my kid wants" Mom who serves Nutella Pringle sandwiches on Wonderbread. Or the "I'll be shipping my kid off to boarding school soon" Mom who has the whole affair catered. Whatever the menu, Mommy discreetly steals food off your *Toy Story 2* plate because for some reason no one ever feeds the grown-ups. Eventually, Mommy has to reciprocate and host the Playdate. This. Blows. Mommy's house is left looking like a Fisher-Price bomb went off in her living room, her Terrapin Green feature wall has been rendered Crayola Corner, and her IKEA cabinetry will never close properly again. The Playdate is also known colloquially as the Sharing of Germs, so Mommy gets to play nursemaid for the forty-eight vomit-filled hours that follow. Yay.

THE PLAYDATE DIGESTIF

INGREDIENTS

1 ounce light rum

4 ounces ginger ale

INSTRUCTIONS

Fill a glass with ice. Pour in the rum and ginger ale,
and stir.

NOTE

The ginger ale will help calm your churning
stomach while you dig half-chewed raisins out of
the living room carpet later that night.

HOW BADLY YOU NEED THIS DRINK

92

CHILDREN'S MUSIC

Mommy's knowledge of contemporary music ended the day you were born. She's praying the "Apple Bottom Jeans" song by Florida (Editor's note: it's "Low" by Flo Rida) becomes a classic ASAP so that her iTunes library will be relevant again. Until then, she'll have to rely on discreetly using Shazam at parties to avoid looking like a complete tool. Wait, is *tool* still cool? (Editor's note: no.) Daddy is no help either because his selection of music is comprised exclusively of early 1980s hair bands. At work, Mommy overheard some twenty-somethings talking about Cee Lo Green and she thought it was an STD. Her iPod is now playlist after playlist of the saccharine sounds of The Wiggles. *Whyyyyyy* do you want to hear the same song over and over and over again? "The Wheels on the Bus" drive Mommy insane, all around the town. Even the *Babies Go Pearl Jam* CD is making her ears bleed. If she has to hear "Even Flow" played on a glockenspiel one more time, she might go crazier than when Jeremy spoke in class today! (Halfhearted high five for quoting lyrics from the album *Ten,* which came out in 1991.) The only time she'll be exposed to new artists now is when they guest perform on *Sesame Street.* Mommy can't wait until you become a teenager so at least she'll know what's hip when she bangs on your door and yells at you to "Turn it down!"

THE RAFFI-TINI

INGREDIENTS

Wedge of lime

Sugar

1 ounce light rum

4 ounces white grape juice

INSTRUCTIONS

Rim a martini glass with a lime wedge and then
sugar. Combine the rum and grape juice in a shaker
with ice. Shake well and strain into the glass. Serve
with Baby Beluga caviar.

HOW BADLY YOU NEED THIS DRINK

93

RESTAURANTS

In a past, hedonistic life, dropping $200 on a menu awash with quail egg, duck-olive paste, and basil-leaf-infused martinis at the hottest new eatery was a surefire remedy for the soul-sucking effects of a fifty-hour workweek. Even though the Calista Flockhart–portion size meant a pizza run three hours later, it was worth it. Adorned with mason jar glassware, chalkboard menus, and beardy servers in skinny jeans, a baby would be as out of place in these bistros as an affordable bottle of wine. Which is why nowadays, on those nights when figuring out a meal plan is as overwhelming as working the Apple TV, Mommy's restaurant criteria have taken a dramatic turn from her pre-baby tastes. Nowadays, parking is mandatory, as are automatic double doors to accommodate the stroller carrying you and half your toy box. Bonus points for a dining area filled with the deafening sounds of a Michael Bolton/Screaming Children mash-up and a menu featuring photos of the entrées. Two minutes after placing their order, Mommy and Daddy's meals arrive so fried they can't tell who ended up with the chicken and who got the fish. No one bats an eye as you fling pieces of your hormone-infused hamburger patty from your high chair and spill milk all over the brown paper tablecloth, dissolving the server's name written in crayon. In fact, most of the parents at surrounding tables just seem thrilled that their own badly behaved child is now sharing the spotlight with you. Even though the only common ingredient between family chain restaurants and hipster hot spots is a shamelessly overpriced menu, walking away from the mess you've left in your wake makes every penny well spent.

TGIF (THANK GOD IT'S FREE.)

(nonalcoholic)

INGREDIENTS

A bottomless glass of fountain cola

NOTE

Free refills = a Mommy do.

HOW BADLY YOU NEED THIS DRINK

MØRNINGS

Before you were born, mornings looked liked this:

7:15 AM: Alarm goes off. Snooze for fifteen minutes.
7:30 AM: Blend a smoothie. Enjoy while surfing Facebook in front of *The Today Show*.
7:45 AM: Take an extralong hot shower. With Daddy.
8:00 AM: Blow-dry and style hair.
8:15 AM: Experiment with a daytime smoky eye look.
8:30 AM: Begin morning subway commute. Listen to a downloaded TED talk.
9:00 AM: Settle into desk and brace for a day of trying to be awesome at everything.

And this is how mornings look now:

6:00 AM: You go off.
6:05 AM: Your entire toy box is now on the floor.
7:05 AM: Your entire breakfast is now on the floor.
8:05 AM: Your entire wardrobe is now on the floor.
8:10 AM: Get showered, dressed, made up, fed, and caffeinated in ten minutes because Daddy has to leave early for another "very important meeting."
8:20 AM: Mommy's entire wardrobe is now on the floor.
8:25 AM: You are having a temper tantrum on the floor.
8:30 AM: Walk you to day care. You burst into hysterical tears upon entering the building.
8:40 AM: Pry you from leg. Mascara ruined.
8:45 AM: Begin morning subway commute. Write a grocery list, reapply mascara, feel guilty, cram for Big Important Meeting, remember six critical things that were not relayed to Daddy about this evening's post–day care logistics.
9:15 AM: Settle into desk and brace for a day of trying to be awesome at everything.

THE RED EYE

(nonalcoholic)

INGREDIENTS

A shot of espresso in a tall mug of regular-brewed
coffee, with sugar to taste

NOTE

Pair with CoverGirl LashBlast
waterproof mascara.

HOW BADLY YOU NEED THIS DRINK

          🍼   🍼   🍼

95

～ WEDDINGS ～

Once upon a time, going to a wedding without a plus one was as excruciating as *The Hangover: Part III*. But tonight, with you in tow, Mommy finds herself staring longingly at the Singles Table. She recalls with fondness an era when the evening's biggest challenge would entail rejecting the advances of the groom's socially awkward cousin. Tonight it's all about keeping you quiet and ensuring your adorable outfit doesn't fall victim to poo leakage, as the only backup attire in the diaper bag is a Onesie imprinted with "I only cry when ugly people hold me" in Comic Sans. Between investing in a "cocktail chic" outfit you'll never wear again and padding her gift envelope with an extra Benjamin, this is turning out to be a very costly affair. Mommy used to take secret comfort in the fact that she would more than pay out her wedding-gift expenditure in Champagne consumption by the night's end. But tonight she'll be lucky if she manages to scarf down two bites of her rubber tofu steak (she ordered salmon), let alone participate in open-bar-fueled shenanigans on the dance floor, which always used to end with Daddy wearing his Hugo Boss tie around his head and screaming "Play Thunderstruck!" Besides, if she and Daddy don't get you back to the hotel room by 8 PM, it will be a contest between you and the bride to see who melts down first. Truthfully, once the cake is cut, Mommy's more than ready to hit the sack after an evening spent whisking you outside every ten minutes and trying to restrain you from throwing macaroons into the mother of the bride's decorative hat. If only Mommy and Daddy were the ones Hawaii bound tomorrow morning.

WEDDING CAKE MARTINI

INGREDIENTS

1½ ounces vanilla vodka

½ ounce coconut rum

1½ ounces pineapple juice

½ ounce cranberry juice

INSTRUCTIONS

Chill a martini glass. Combine all the ingredients in a
shaker with ice. Shake well and strain into the glass.

NOTE

Missed the wedding cake? Don't despair. All the
taste and zero mess. Just say yes!

HOW BADLY YOU NEED THIS DRINK

96

OTHER KIDS

Mommy firmly believes you are exhibiting early signs of genius and are destined to solve the world's dependence on oil or win the *Jeopardy!* Tournament of Champions. The problem is other parents *also* feel that way about their own kids, even though clearly some of the graduating class from this reach-for-the-middle generation will be your future employees. Their behavior is a reflection of questionable child-rearing approaches, like the "let my kid do whatever while I check my stocks on my smartphone" method. Mommy passes judgment silently from the sidelines of the sandbox (or very vocally when she's had wine with Daddy). Although socialization is key to your development, the following toddler types should be avoided whenever possible:

The Biter: No one wants baby rabies. Does BabyBjörn make a muzzle?

The Screamer: Exacerbates Mommy's permanent postnatal headache.

The Crier: Even a light breeze results in tears.

The Suck: Always clinging. No adult conversation possible. Cut the umbilical cord!

The Bully: Pushes, grabs, yells, steals. Future drug dealer or investment banker.

The Show Kid: Needs to be center of attention at all times. Has a British accent?

The Germ Harborer: Just gross.

The Perfect Angel: Also to be avoided. Should you cry, scream, break things, or do anything else a normal toddler does, the Perfect Angel's mother will lose her shit.

THE PERFECT MARTINI

INGREDIENTS

2 ounces gin

Splash of dry vermouth

Twist of lemon

INSTRUCTIONS

Chill a martini glass. Combine the gin and vermouth
in a shaker with ice. Shake well and strain into the
glass. Garnish with a lemon twist. Drink in honor of
your Perfect Angel, whom other parents are judging
behind your back.

HOW BADLY YOU NEED THIS DRINK

97

OTHER MOMMIES

Much like there are certain toddlers who should be avoided whenever possible, so are there red-flag Mommy types:

The Biter: Sleep deprivation has taken its toll on this caustic Mommy. Even comments about the weather are interpreted as a personal attack on her parenting method.

The Screamer: Can someone please anonymously send this woman a copy of *The Baby Whisperer*?

The Crier: "Being a parent is just (*sniff*) like so amazing, you know?"

The Suck: Her incessant whining about lack of sleep, financial woes, and laundry is sucking Mommy's will to live. P.S., *We're all in the same boat!*

The Bully: Regularly clad in a "Breast is Best" T-shirt, she gets her high off shoving Dr. Sears down other Mommies' throats while shoving mini-quiches down hers.

The Show Mom: Constantly brags about her child's walk-on role in local car dealership commercial. Always dissatisfied with head-shot photographers in this city. Has a British accent?

The Germ Harborer: Just gross.

The problem is, Mommy falls into at least three of these categories on any given day, depending on which way the hormonal winds happen to be blowing, which is probably why her in-box is no longer overflowing with playdate invitations.

MARCO SOLO

(nonalcoholic)

INGREDIENTS

¾ ounce lemon juice

½ ounce grenadine

½ ounce simple syrup

Lemon-lime soda

Soda water

INSTRUCTIONS

Fill a glass with ice. Pour in the lemon juice,
grenadine, and simple syrup. Top off with equal parts
of lemon-lime soda and soda water.

NOTE

Socially acceptable to consume alone.

HOW BADLY YOU NEED THIS DRINK

98

MOMMY NIGHTS OUT

Mommy and her girlfriends decide it's time to pay tribute to their single days by delegating child care to the Daddies and painting the town red. Emails about logistics flood Mommy's in-box for three weeks leading up to the event, but as the big night approaches the cancellations come rolling in. Friend 1 is "coming down with something" (read: *Dirty Dancing* is on TBS). Friend 2 is having a breakdown because nothing in her closet fits and fears she would just be a buzzkill (true). And Friend 3's kid is projectile vomiting (again). The few left standing amp things up to compensate for the no-shows ("Let's do Jägerbombs like it's 2009!"). Owing to a lack of tolerance from their leave of absence from life, this results in drunken overshares about marital sex (eew) and Moms Gone Wild antics like not immediately answering Daddy's voice mail asking where the Cheetos are. Cut to 6 AM. Getting up with you only four hours after Mommy rolled in is a painful reminder that things have changed since those estrogen-charged nights of years past, but the flurry of photo tags, hangover war stories, and "Has anyone seen my glasses?" texts that transpire over her phone in the hours that follow happily remind her that some things always stay the same.

MOMMY'S HELPER

(nonalcoholic)

INGREDIENTS

½ cup spinach

1 banana

½ cup soy milk

½ cup chopped ice

3 drops vitamin B_{12}

INSTRUCTIONS

Combine all the ingredients in a blender and blend until smooth. Pour into a tall glass. Consume immediately.

NOTE

Pairs well with a greasy breakfast prepared by Daddy.

HOW BADLY YOU NEED THIS DRINK

99

_____ ✑ VACATIONS ✑ _____

Mommy and Daddy are pasty, overworked, and painfully aware that your second birthday is fast approaching, at which time you will (*gasp!*) no longer fly free. Thus, it's time to book a family vacation. The temptation to go somewhere exotic is immediately quashed because Mommy needs to be assured that the local hospital isn't out of the back of a van and that the chief of surgery isn't also the head bartender. Not to mention the food can't give anyone dysentery—you've got enough coming out of your back end when you drink safe Brita-filtered water. So they do what everyone with kids does: go to Florida. Hooray for the continental United States, where there's a Starbucks on every corner. Mommy books a family-friendly room that comes equipped with a Pack 'n Play, which unfortunately won't fit in the bathroom. (It's not like you'll remember sleeping next to a toilet. Mommy just really wanted to shut the door!) The flight is a nightmare, the car rental "forgot" to include a car seat with the Ford Escape, and owing to absolutely no time change, you're somehow completely thrown off your nap schedule for the entire week. Also, why did they choose a destination that requires sunscreen twenty-four hours a day and is nowhere near the ocean? Oh, because of Disney World, where dreams do come true. Or nightmares. After blowing the basement repair fund on this vacation, Mommy realizes the theme park is completely age inappropriate and Mickey scares the crap out of you. Literally. All over the Magic Kingdom. The only activity Mommy and Daddy can really enjoy is shopping the outlet malls, where they end up spending another small fortune on baby sunhats and Wetzel's Pretzels. At the end of it all, Mommy needs a vacation from her vacation. At least, unlike vacations from her single days, this time she doesn't fear she's coming home with an STD.

STAYCATION LIBATION

INGREDIENTS

1 ounce light rum

2 ounces orange juice

½ ounce simple syrup

Splash of lime juice

Dash of grenadine

Fresh mint leaves

INSTRUCTIONS

Combine the rum, orange juice, simple syrup, lime juice, and grenadine in a shaker with ice. Shake well and strain into a tall ice-filled glass. Garnish with mint and a mini-umbrella. Crank up the heat and stay home.

HOW BADLY YOU NEED THIS DRINK

_l YOU'RE GROWING UP TOO FAST _l

You're eighteen months old. You're healthy, happy, and, by some miracle of miracles, Mommy and Daddy managed not to break you. Though you do have a few bumps and bruises from learning to walk and whacking your head every time you crawl under the coffee table, all and all Mommy is pretty impressed that you've reached the toddler stage relatively unscathed. You've got a big toothy grin, you're saying a few key words (unfortunately, *no* is becoming your favorite), and your heartfelt belly laugh makes Mommy's heart explode. Although Mommy does have a pit of fear in her stomach for what lies ahead, like potty training and the terrible twos, she's truly in love with this stage you're in now. Could she do it again? As she looks back on your 298,076 baby pictures (actual number), her ovaries clang with nostalgia for the sweet smell of milk on your breath and those wriggling little toes. Nature has a magical way of erasing the sleepless nights, the colicky screams, and nipple pain from a mother's memory. And it would be pretty special to watch you become a role model to a little brother or sister. Maybe Mommy and Daddy should crack open a bottle of wine and throw caution, and condoms, to the wind. That is, after all, how they ended up here in the first place.

①

THE KOOL-AID

NOTE

Go ahead and drink it.
Being a Mommy is the best.

HOW BADLY YOU NEED THIS DRINK

🍼 🍼 🍼 🍼 🍼

ACKNOWLEDGMENTS

LYRANDA MARTIN EVANS:

To my parents, who after five kids and more than forty years of marriage are still very much in love. You've set the benchmark for outstanding parenting—always loving us unconditionally, pushing us to reach our full potential, and never picking a favorite (*cough*). To my brothers and sisters, you inspire me every day to be The Beast. And finally, to Paul Constable, who helped push the comedy of this book like a magic frog without a byline, you gave me PJMC and I am eternally grateful.

FIONA STEVENSON:

Thank you to my husband, Hadley, who is the best friend/partner/co-parent I could ever begin to imagine. I can't believe I get to wake up every day to someone so generous, compassionate, hilarious, and fun. Thank you to my incredible mom and siblings for constantly motivating me, for surrounding my new family and me with unconditional love, and for being an endless source of inspiration, support, and laughter. You are the best!

LYRANDA AND FIONA:

Carolyn Forde at Westwood Creative Artists. Anna Thompson at Three Rivers Press. Moira Stevenson. Charlotte Empey and Metro News.

To our insanely awesome friends, who supported us through our Red and Grey high school years, our Very Special Shoes: Remount, our Tri-color university days, our critically acclaimed (by the four people in the audience) Math is Hard sketch shows, our Schmooze glory days, new parenthood, and this Le Café III project.

Tina Constable, Mauro DiPreta, Campbell Wharton, Tammy Blake, Meredith McGinnis, Linda Kaplan, Sigi Nacson, Elizabeth Rendfleisch, Maria Elias, and Travis Cowdy.

And every person who read our blog and shared, commented, tweeted, and laughed in solidarity with every mushy pea flung on the floor.

DRINK INDEX

Ale
 The Florence Nightin-ale, 77
Amaretto
 Alabama Slammer, 155
 An Orgasm, 53

Blue curaçao
 The Bugablue, 187
 The Pool Party, 101
Bourbon
 "Don't Fertilize My Egg!" Nog,
  135
 The Warm Welcome, 35

Coffee liqueur
 Brown Cow, 125
 The Mad Cow, 159
 Mexican Coffee, 55
Crème de cacao
 The After Eight, 175
 The Pearly Gate, 167

Gin
 The Aviator, 103
 Coco Chanel, 71
 The Dubonnet Cocktail, 191
 Hair of the Dog, 59
 J.T.'s G&T, 69
 Keep the Peace, 61
 Nap Thyme, 115

Off the Rails, 73
The Perfect Martini, 209
Singapore Sling, 47

Irish cream
 The Brain Cocktail, 95
 Creamy Caramel Appletini, 165
 One-Hit Wonder, 141
 The Supermodel's Nightmare,
  129

Melon liqueur
 The Brain Freeze, 79
 The Layaway, 131
 Zen Cocktail, 45

Nonalcoholic drinks
 Baby Belly-ni, 21
 The Birth Announcement, 27
 The Confetti Cocktail, 157
 The Due Date, 19
 Fountain of Youth, 185
 Knocked Up in a Cup, 49
 The Lonely Island, 149
 Marco Solo, 211
 Minibar Mocktini, 117
 Mommy's Helper, 213
 The Red Eye, 205
 The Safe Traveler, 39
 The Self-Restraint, 87

The "Wish You Were A" Virgin
  Mary, 23

Pimms
  The Welcome Mat, 105

Rum
  The Celebri-tini, 65
  Day Care Defense, 193
  The Grown-Up Goblet, 163
  A Hurrycane, 93
  Liquid Drano, 145
  Parentiña Colada, 147
  Parks and Wreck, 183
  The Playdate Digestif, 199
  The Raffi-tini, 201
  The Seven-Day Weekend, 57
  The Shopping Maul, 81
  Staycation Libation, 215
  A Zombie, 123
Rye
  A Man-hattan, 139
  Off the Rails, 73

Scotch
  Walk 'n' Roll, 179
Southern Comfort
  The Home Invasion, 195

Tequila
  Career Suicide, 173
  Mockingbird, 31
  The Silver Scream, 37

Vodka
  Amazon Lemonade, 171
  The Bloody Mary Poppins, 137
  The Box Office Smash, 67
  China White, 83
  The Cool Crowd Cappuccino,
    133
  The Cosmompolitan, 143
  The Doctor's Order, 153
  Gold Medal Cocktail, 189
  The In-Flight Cocktail, 127
  Insta-Graham Shot, 151
  Mommy Monitor System, 181
  A Mudslide, 75
  A Salty Dog, 89
  Screwdriver, 121
  The Sideswipe, 107
  The Skinny Bitch, 85
  Wedding Cake Martini, 207

Whisky
  Board Book Empire, 169
Wine / sparkling wine
  The Friend Request, 97
  The Ghosts of Boyfriends Past,
    91
  The Ironic Cocktail, 161
  Luxury Libation, 113
  Red Carpet Fizz, 63
  The Stepford Spritzer, 41

SUBJECT INDEX

Abstinence, 32

Aging, 184

Babies
  celebrity, 64
  checking on, 180
  choosing name for, 26
  fevers and colds, 76
  first days at home, 24
  growth spurts, 108
  hair-pulling, 148
  sleep schedules, 54, 86, 114
  younger sibling for, 140
Baby carriers, 46
Baby showers, 18
Babysitters, 110
Bath time, 144
Board books, 168
Boyfriends (ex), 90
Breast-feeding, 28, 124, 158
Brunch, 132

Car seats, 38
Celebrity moms, 62
Clothing, 80, 108, 118, 128

Daddy, 138, 184
Day care, 192
Diaper bags, 70
Diapers, 112

Facebook, 96, 150
Flying, 102

Gadgets, 164
Global warming, 98
Grandparents, 60, 190
Grocery shopping, 170
Gym memberships, 176

Hair, 58
Haircuts, 160
Hangovers, 212
Holidays, 134
Home renovations, 120
Homes, baby proofing, 154
Homes, buying, 104
Hormones, 68
Hotels, 116
Houseguests, 194

Income, disposable, 130
In-laws, 60

Labor, 22, 66
Laundry, 118

Meal planning, 146
Mommy Brain, 78, 168
Mommy Fear (MF), 196
Mommy groups, 40

Mommy Nights Out, 212
Morning routines, 204
Movie theaters, 36
Music, children's, 200

Nannies, 136
Neighbors, 104
Nursery, 30

Parenting methods, 208, 210
Parks and playgrounds, 182
Parties, childrens', 156
Partying, 42, 212
Pediatricians, 152
Pets, 88
Photos, 134, 150, 184
Playdates, 198
Poop, 74
Pregnancy, perks of, 48
Prenatal classes, 20
Public transportation, 72
Pumping, 124

Restaurants, 202

Sex, 52
Sick days, 50

Single people, 142
Sippy cups, 162
Sleep deprivation, 54, 174
Spa visits, 44
Sports, 188
Strollers, 186
Swim class, 100
Symmetry, body, 106

Teething, 166
Toddlers
    badly behaved, 208
    bedtimes, 174
    celebrating, 216
Toys, 82
TV, 94

Vacations, 214
Visitors, 34, 194

Walking, 178
Weaning, 158
Weather, 92
Weddings, 206
Workplace, 56, 122, 126, 172

Yoga, 84

ABOUT THE AUTHORS

LYRANDA MARTIN EVANS is an award-winning advertising copy-writer who is currently a creative director at one of Canada's top advertising agencies. She writes and performs sketch comedy, and her former life as a bartender informs the book's delicious drink recipes. FIONA STEVENSON is an award-winning brand marketer and innovation consultant who is also frequently leveraged as a corporate host. She is a trained improviser, and writes and performs sketch comedy. TOGETHER, they are the creators of the popular blog *Reasons Mommy Drinks*.

Follow *Reasons Mommy Drinks* at Facebook.com/reasonsmommy drinks and Twitter@mommyreasons.